# Work Of Art, A Love So Smart

### 50 River Beneath 50 Ocean

## Season Of Obsession
## Vol. 1

## CHANDAN MALANA

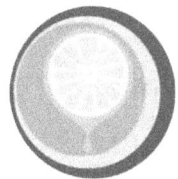

### Chandan Malana Publication House

**ISBN:  9798857834466**

Cover design by:
**Chandan Malana**

Published by
**Chandan Malana
Publication House**

# Preface

In the realm of human emotions, obsession is a force both captivating and bewildering. It dances on the fine line between passion and possession, love and fixation. "Work Of Art, A Love So Smart," authored by Chandan Malana, delves deep into this intricate web of feelings, presenting a collection of poems and quotes that explore the multifaceted nature of obsession.

Obsession, like a double-edged sword, can cut through the fabric of rationality, blurring the boundaries between desire and compulsion. With eloquence and sensitivity, Chandan Malana's words unravel the stories of hearts ensnared by an irresistible force, a love that defies conventions and expectations. Through the medium of poetry and thought-provoking quotes, this book delves into the intensity of human emotions, revealing the hidden corners of the soul where passion takes root.

In "Work Of Art, A Love So Smart," each verse is a brushstroke that paints the canvas of obsession with its hues of longing, vulnerability, and surrender. The author's exploration of this complex theme goes beyond the surface, peeling back the layers of the human psyche to expose the raw and authentic emotions that fuel our most intense desires. Whether it's the obsession that fuels an artist's creativity, the love that consumes a heart, or the yearning that refuses to be silenced, these pages offer a profound journey through the labyrinth of human yearning.

As you embark on this literary voyage, prepare to be captivated by the evocative imagery, the lyrical beauty, and the depth of emotion that Chandan Malana weaves into every line. "Work Of Art, A Love So Smart" is not merely a collection of poems and quotes—it is a mirror that reflects the myriad shades of obsession, inviting readers to confront their own desires, vulnerabilities, and dreams.

May these verses ignite your imagination, awaken your emotions, and resonate with the intimate experiences that make us human. Let the words on these pages remind you that obsession, with all its complexities, is a testament to the profound capacity of the human heart to love and to be moved by the exquisite work of art that is life itself.

# Message From Author

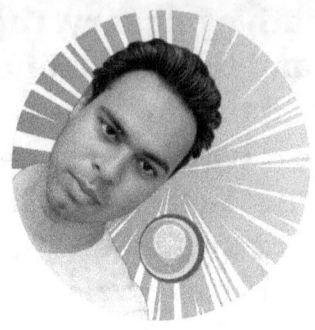

## B.Sc Bioinformatics
## M.Sc Microbiology
## PG.Diploma In Aroma Technology

## Dear Readers,

I am Chandan Malana, the author of the book "Work Of Art, A Love So Smart". This book has 50 Obsession poetic masterpieces and 50 Obsessed quotes. It is the first volume of the series "Season Of Obsession".

Writing poetry has been my hobby since my school days, and it has grown into a passionate pastime. I am very proud and excited to finally share my work with you.

If you enjoy this book, I would love to publish a second volume. Please feel free to contact me at any time with your feedback, comments, and suggestions.

Thank you for your support!

Best regards,

Chandan Malana

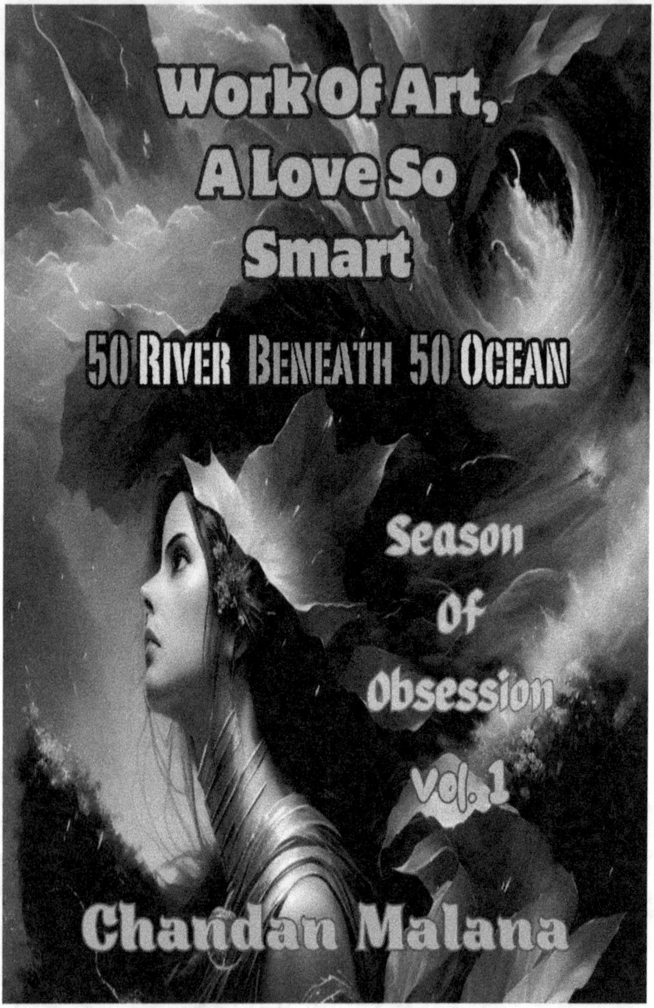

# Work Of Art, A Love So Smart

## 50 River Beneath 50 Ocean

Season Of Obsession Vol. 1

## Chandan Malana

Chandan Malana Publication House

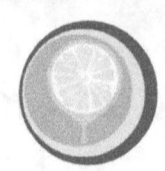

# Contents

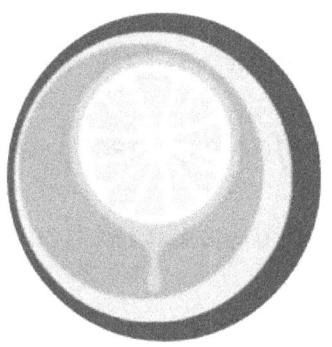

# Admirers March, Led By Inner Force

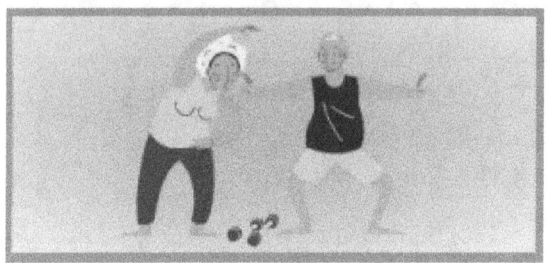

Obsession's grip, relentless and strong,

In the symphony of fate, it plays along.

Guided by forces, unseen and divine,

Destiny weaves its intricate design.

In every step, a predetermined trace,

As souls entwine in this cosmic embrace.

No mere coincidence, this grand affair,

A tapestry of love, woven with care.

The admirers that gather, drawn by the thread,

Bound by the path that destiny has spread.

Their hearts' compass guided by unseen hands,

To cross your path, fulfilling fate's demands.

Through time and space, they journey afar,

Drawn by the light of destiny's star.

In the script of life, they play their part,

Forever entwined, linked by fate's art.


Obsession's flame, an all-consuming fire,

Driven by fate's unyielding desire.

Through trials and challenges, they remain,

For destiny's hand, they cannot restrain.

In the darkest night or the brightest day,

Fate's decree leads admirers your way.

They're bound by a force they can't comprehend,

A love that transcends, with no need to pretend.




So cherish those souls fate has brought near,

For their presence in your life is clear.

Embrace the divine, for it has conspired,

To unite hearts in a love so admired.

Fate's pen has written, its ink forever set,

An eternal bond, destiny won't forget.

Embrace the journey, guided by the divine,

For fate's design is yours and yours to define.


*Chandan Malana*

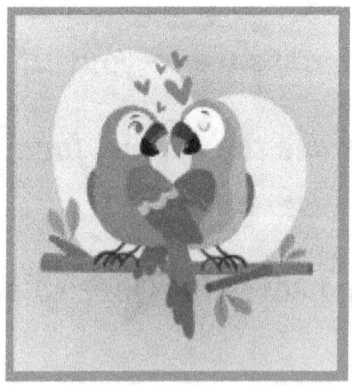

# Quote 1

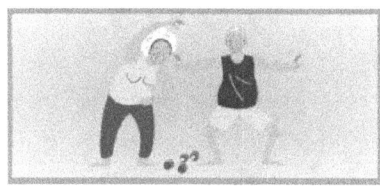

"Destiny and fate, a divine hand in play, Not just coincidence, as they say, Admirers brought by an unseen force's sway, Bound by a purpose that time cannot sway."

Chandan Malana

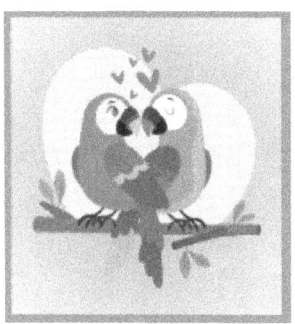

# Beyond Words And Vows

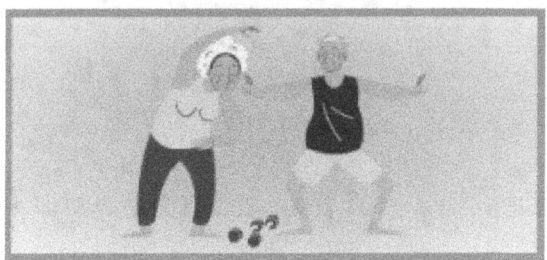

Where love and obsession intertwine,

No oaths or promises need we bind.

For in their fervent embrace, we find,

A passion that transcends the confines.

In the depths of hearts consumed by fire,

Love's flame burns with an intense desire.

Obsession's grip, relentless and dire,

Yet in their fusion, souls never tire.



No need for words, no need to proclaim,

For their connection is never the same.

Love's gentle whispers drown out all blame,

Obsession's hold, like a sacred flame.

They dance in harmony, two souls entwined,

Love's symphony, with obsession aligned.

No need for oaths, no need for a signed,

For their bond withstands the test of time.


In every touch, a thousand stories unfold,

Love's caress, obsession's grip takes hold.

No need for promises, no need to be told,

Their love's tale, a masterpiece untold.

Where love and obsession unite as one,

A cosmic force, a love never undone.

No need for vows, their hearts have
already won,

Their souls intertwined beneath the
same sun.


In their passion's embrace, they soar
high,

Love's wings, obsession's flame reaches
the sky.

No need for pledges, no need to comply,

Their devotion speaks without a reply.

Where love and obsession both reside,

No oaths or promises need they
confide.

For in their union, they forever abide,

A love beyond measure, forever tied.

Chandan Malana

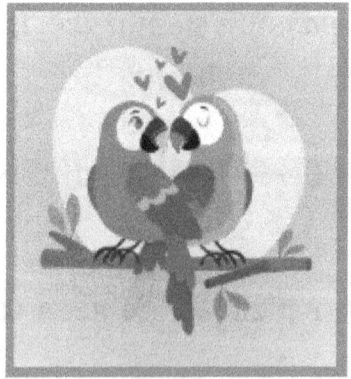

# Quote 2

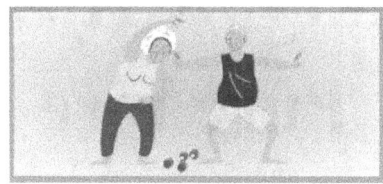

"In the presence of love and obsession hold, Oaths and promises are but tales untold, For the heart beats true, and passion is bold, A love like this, cannot be bought or sold."

Chandan Malana

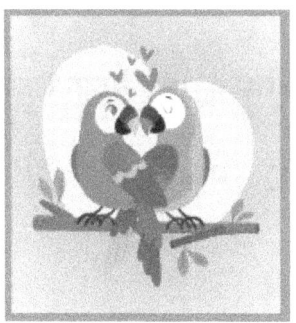

# Captivated By Beauty: A Heart's Pure Fire

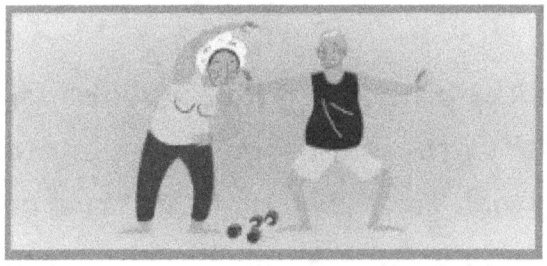

*Even now, your allure enchants my sight,*

*A breathtaking symphony of pure delight.*

*In every glance, my heart skips a beat,*

*Obsessed by your beauty, it's a love so sweet.*

I stand in awe as your radiance shines,

An ethereal glow, divine and sublime.

Your presence consumes my every thought,

An obsession unyielding, an obsession unsought.


Each curve, each line, a masterpiece defined,

A work of art, with no flaws to find.

Your beauty, a riddle I long to unravel,

A captivating spell I willingly travel.

Lost in the depths of your mesmerizing
eyes,

I drown in their depths, where love
never dies.

The luster of your skin, so soft and
pure,

An obsession that lingers, an allure so
sure.


Your voice, a melody that soothes my
soul,

A siren's song, an intoxicating control.

I'm spellbound by your words, your
every tone,

Obsessed with your presence, I am
yours alone.

The way you move, a dance so grace,

Each step, a rhythm, I eagerly embrace.

Your elegance, a magnet that pulls me
near,

An obsession that grows, year after
year.




Your laughter, a symphony of joy and
glee,

A sound that sets my restless heart
free.

In your presence, my worries all
subside,

Obsessed with your happiness, forever
by your side.

*Even now, your beauty remains my muse,*

*A source of inspiration, never to lose.*

*In this world of chaos, you're my sanctuary,*

*An eternal obsession, my beloved, my extraordinary.*

**Chandan Malana**

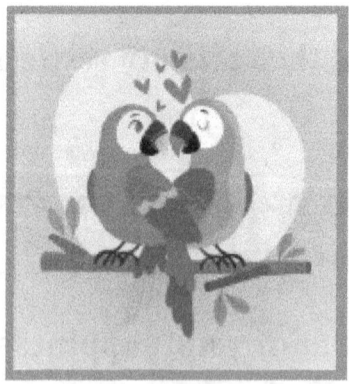

# Quote 3

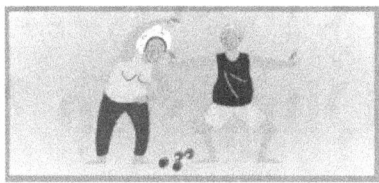

*"Enchanted by your timeless allure, My heart races, my passions pure. Lost in wonder at your beauty grand, My soul captivated, held in your hand."*

Chandan Malana

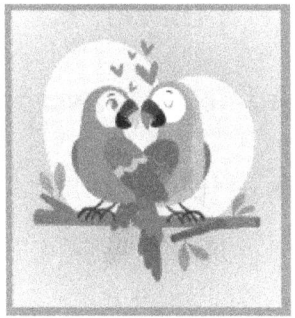

# Charmed By Love, Or Locked In Its Obsession ?

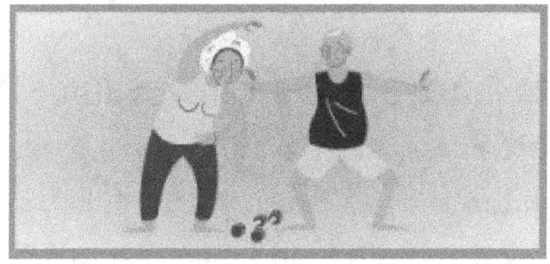

Was this the peak of passion's fiery blaze,

Or just the throes of madness in a haze?

In every shadow cast, I saw your grace,

Obsession's grip tightening with each embrace.

A tender touch, a whisper in my ear,

Your essence consumed me, my heart held dear.

But was it love that fueled this wild desire,

Or the depths of madness, set my soul on fire?


In dreams, your image danced before my eyes,

A haunting beauty, no escape could provide.

I sought your presence in every waking hour,

Lost in the depths of love's consuming power.

I yearned to hold you close, to feel your
skin,

To drown within your love, let passion
win.

But was it love that led me down this
path,

Or madness clouding reason's
aftermath?

I traced your face in every star above,

Believed in love's eternal, boundless
love.

Yet doubts crept in, my sanity to test,

Were these sweet dreams or delusions
at best?

A *prisoner* to desire, my heart
confined,

Obsession's chains, a madness
intertwined.

I craved your presence, your touch,
your embrace,

But was it love's essence or my mind's
embrace?

The line blurred between devotion and
madness,

As love's sweet symphony turned into
sadness.

I questioned if this love was real or not,

Or just the echoes of a mind
distraught.

And so I pondered, trapped within this haze,

Caught between love's ecstasy and its maze.

Was this the limit of love or my madness,

A question lingering in the depths of darkness.

Chandan Malana

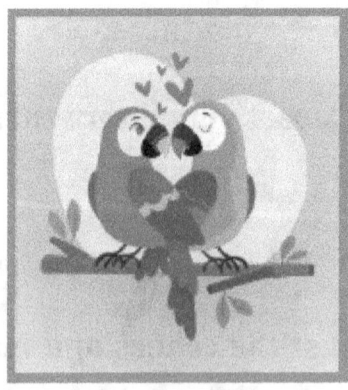

# Quote 4

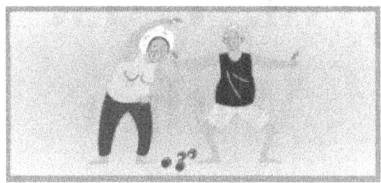

"A query springs forth, was it love or obsession, As your face appears in every form and possession. My heart races, yet my mind remains in wonder, With every thought of you, my feelings pierce like thunder."

Chandan Malana

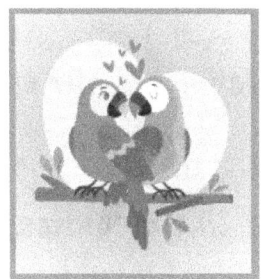

# Deception's Charm, Trust Lies Within

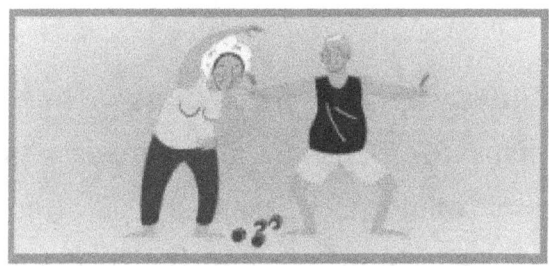

*In a world of falsehoods, we stand amazed,*

*For your deceptive words have us entranced.*

*With blind devotion, our trust we have raised,*

*Your lies, like melodies, sweetly enhanced.*

Oh, master of deception, we're beguiled,

Enraptured by the webs you skillfully spin.

In admiration, our hearts have been styled,

Lost in the labyrinth, where truth grows thin.


Your promises, like whispered fantasies,

We cling to them, enchanted and enthralled.

With fervent faith, we ignore discrepancies,

Ignoring warning signs, we're yet enthralled.

A twisted dance, this game of hide and seek,

As we chase illusions, your lies take flight.

Blinded by obsession, we're naive and meek,

Unfazed by the darkness concealed from sight.



Each falsehood spoken, a stroke of your art,

Painting a portrait of a world untrue.

Ensnared by the charm, we play our part,

Consumed by love for the lies we pursue.

In this masquerade, we willingly dance,

Delighting in the masks you deftly wear.

No hint of doubt, no inkling of a chance,

That beneath it all, deceit lies ensnared.


Oh, how we yearn for truth, yet fail to see,

The tangled web you weave so skillfully.

In our obsession, we remain unfree,

Bound to your lies, forever willingly.

But in the depths of our infatuation,

A whisper lingers, a faint note of doubt.

Will we awaken from this fascination,

Or forever in your lies, be devout?

Chandan Malana

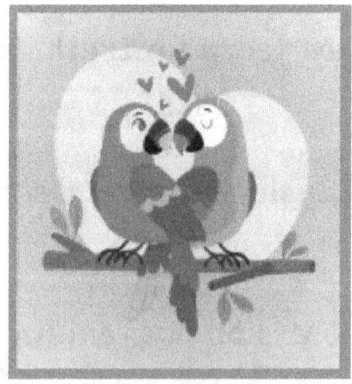

# Quote 5

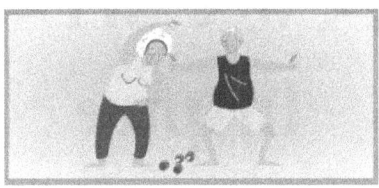

"Lies of trust, we do not spurn, For your words we eagerly yearn. Admiration and love, our hearts unchained, Your words forever etched, our loyalty gained."

Chandan Malana

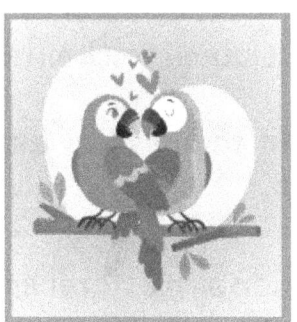

# Destined To Find, A Love Set To Inspire

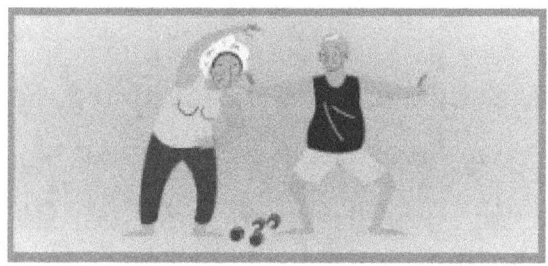

I yearn to tread the path of love's
divine,

To find her waiting, her heart
entwined with mine.

Through meadows fair and valleys
deep,

My passion's fire, forever to keep.

A burning desire consumes my soul,

To reach the destination where love's
seeds are sown.

In dreams and waking hours, she's my
obsession,

Her presence a constant, unyielding
possession.


I chase her shadow through the darkest
night,

Guided by the stars' soft, shimmering
light.

With every step, my heart beats fast,

Closer to her love, a destiny steadfast.

Across oceans wide, I'll brave the
stormy seas,

For love's sweet destination is where I
aim to be.

No mountain too high, no distance too
far,

My passion's flame, an eternal guiding
star.

Her touch, like silk, ignites a fervent
flame,

In her arms, I find solace and no
shame.

The destination of love, a sacred place,

Where our souls entwine, in eternal
embrace.

I'll cross deserts vast, endure the scorching heat,

Driven by love's fervor, a relentless beat.

For in her eyes, I glimpse paradise,

Where desires meet and true love lies.


Through trials and tests, my spirit remains strong,

In pursuit of love's destination, I belong.

With unwavering devotion, I press on,

To find her waiting, where love's essence is drawn.

Oh, sweet destination of love, I draw near,

My heart ablaze, casting aside every fear.

For in that sacred space, where passion thrives,

I'll find her waiting, our souls destined to survive.

**Chandan Malana**

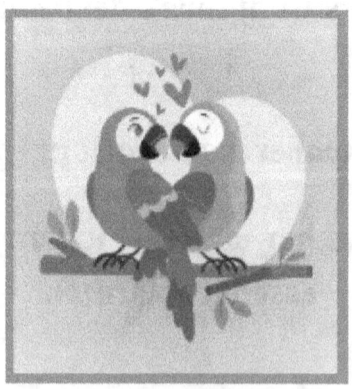

# Quote 6

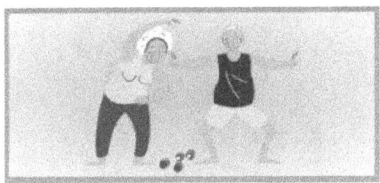

"With steadfast heart and passionate fire, I journey on, my heart's desire. To find the place where love resides, And meet my beloved by my side."

Chandan Malana

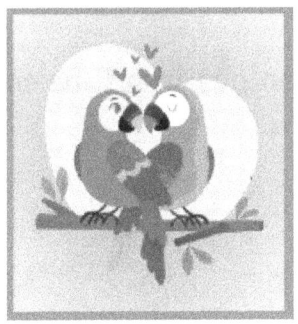

# Divine Obsession

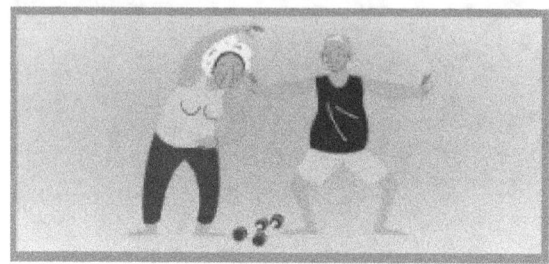

In realms divine, where spirits soar
free,

A love unfolds, obsessed with me.

For even gods, with powers untold,

Find solace in a love so bold.

I am the muse, the cherished flame,

That ignites the heavens with its name.

No mortal heart can claim my soul,

For I belong to a higher goal.


Within my essence, a sacred fire,

An obsession burns with deep desire.

To possess me, a futile quest,

For my heart is divinely blessed.

In passion's dance, I stand apart,

A vessel of love, a work of art.

No earthly chains can bind my will,

For I am free, my spirit's thrill.


The divine whispers, in hallowed voice,

Their obsession with me, the ultimate
choice.

I am their masterpiece, their chosen
one,

In their adoration, my spirit is spun.

I guard my heart, a treasure divine,

Not to be owned by mortal twine.

For I am sacred, a love untamed,

In the realm of obsession, I am named.


No mortal's touch can claim my soul,

For my devotion is to a higher goal.

In the arms of gods, I find release,

A love that transcends, bringing inner
peace.

So let them wonder, let them yearn,

For the love that in my essence churns.

I am not theirs, nor ever shall be,

For the divine obsession is solely for
me.

**Chandan Malana**

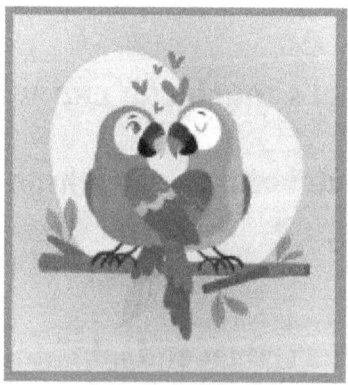

# Quote 7

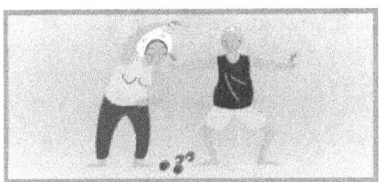

"My spirit and soul belong to the divine, An obsession so deep, it's hard to define, No one else can claim me as their own, I am whole with the divine alone."

Chandan Malana

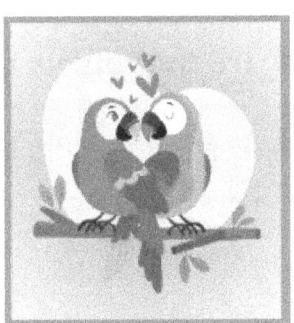

# Dreams That Flicker And Fade

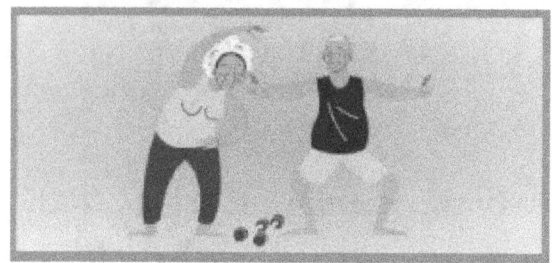

Life is too short, a fleeting span,

Where dreams are born and quickly
banned.

Love, a fire that burns within,

Obsession takes hold, a passionate sin.

In the depths of desire, it thrives,

A relentless pursuit, where reason dies.

It consumes the heart, like a raging
flame,

Leaving no room for logic or shame.


Obsession blinds us, distorts our view,

As we chase the unreachable, the
untrue.

We lose ourselves in its endless maze,

Trading sanity for a transient craze.

But beware, for love can deceive,

A masquerade that many believe.

What once brought joy now brings despair,

Obsession's grip, too heavy to bear.


Life's too short to be consumed,

By a passion that leaves us bruised.

Find balance and let love be kind,

Freeing the heart and soothing the mind.

Seek not the obsession, the
all-consuming,

But love that's gentle,
life-illuminating.

For in the brevity of our mortal stay,

True joy is found in a love that won't
fray.

Embrace the moments, cherish the
days,

Let not obsession lead you astray.

Life's too short to be held in its snare,

Choose love that's real, handle with
care.

*So let us learn from life's fleeting sight,*

*To love with wisdom, to love what's right.*

*For in the end, when our time is through,*

*Love's true essence will carry us through.*

**Chandan Malana**

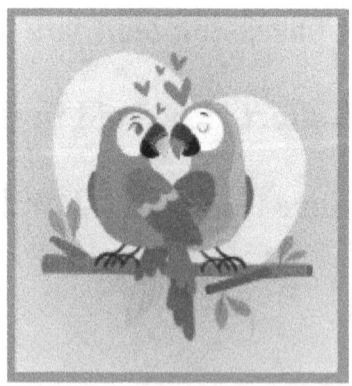

# Quote 8

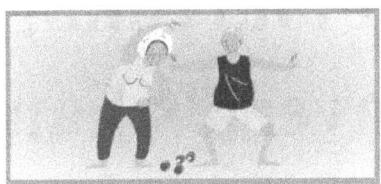

"Love with abandon, yet hold with care, Embrace every moment, with passion to share. For love is a flame, that must be fed, To burn bright and true, 'til the end we're led."

Chandan Malana

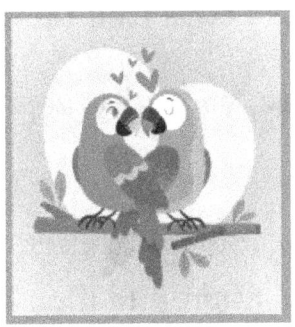

# Enigmatic Grace, Flourishing Tavern's Fame

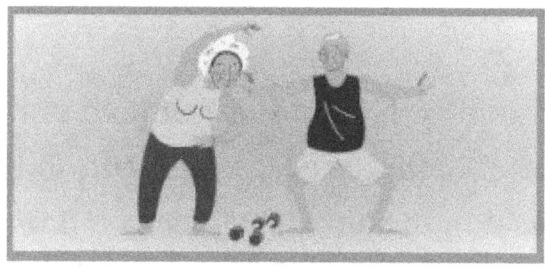

Your apathy, a shield, has guarded the tavern's grace,

If your gaze embraced wine, where would the cups find their place?

Indifference, your ally, kept desires at bay,

But within, a longing stirs, persistent night and day.

A silent spectator, you observe the
revelry,

Yet deep within your heart, a burning
jealousy.

The laughter and the mirth, they dance
before your eyes,

As your own desires yearn for a taste
of paradise.

The tavern's walls bear witness to your
hidden thirst,

But you remain untouched, as if under
a curse.

Each glass, a whispered secret, luring
you to partake,

Yet your indifference persists, an
obsession you can't shake.

The wine, a temptress, entwined in tales untold,

Its crimson hue enticing, its allure manifold.

But you, a distant wanderer, immune to its spell,

With each passing moment, your heart aches and swells.


The tavern's patrons revel, oblivious to your plight,

While you linger in the shadows, hidden from their sight.

But deep within your soul, a fire slowly burns,

For the wine that you deny, your heart forever yearns.

The melodies of joy, they echo through the air,

But your heart remains untouched, burdened by despair.

Oh, if you had embraced the wine, tasted its sweet embrace,

Perhaps the cups would sing of a different time and place.


Yet your indifference holds, a fortress made of stone,

As the tavern's secrets whisper, enticing you to atone.

Your obsession with restraint, a choice you can't undo,

But the longing in your eyes betrays the wine's pull on you.

And so the tavern thrives, a sanctuary
for desire,

While your indifference shields you,
fueling an inner fire.

But deep within your heart, a question
still remains,

If you had drunk the wine, would it
free you from these chains?

Chandan Malana

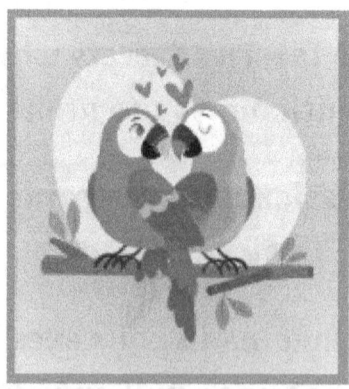

# Quote 9

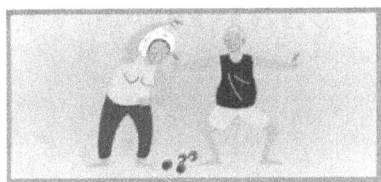

"The majesty of the tavern still remains, Saved by the aloofness that love detains, Yet, had you drank with your own eyes, The wine's ecstasy would've claimed its prize."

*Chandan Malana*

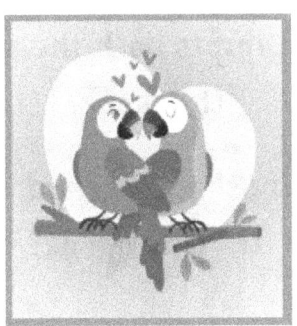

# Fear Of Losing Obsession's Hold

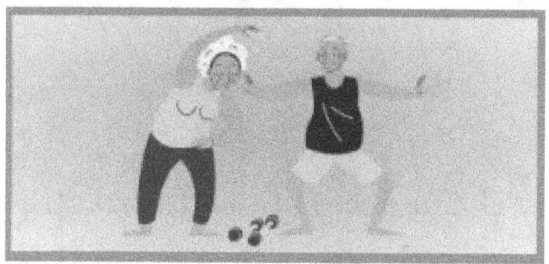

Obsession, a puzzle of the mind's domain,

Entwines the hearts, igniting a fervent flame.

Its allure tempts both the seeker and the meek,

For even those untouched, its power they do speak.

A mystifying force, obsession's embrace,

Binds souls tightly, leaving no trace of grace.

The yearning for what's coveted, undefined,

Leads us on a quest, our sanity confined.


The one consumed by passion's swirling tide,

Fears naught but the loss of what's kept inside.

Yet even those who've never felt its sting,

Tremble in the thought of its absent ring.

The lover yearns to hold their
cherished prize,

To feel their presence, never
compromise.

But fear encroaches, whispering its
doubts,

A constant reminder of love's fragile
bouts.


The artist, too, with brush and canvas
set,

Creates masterpieces, each stroke a
duet.

Yet in their pursuit, anxiety resides,

A fear of losing inspiration's tide.

Obsession knows no boundaries, nor does it spare,

Both the mighty and the meek in its snare.

For even the scholar, consumed by their quest,

Fears losing knowledge, the ultimate bequest.


So let us tread with caution, hearts aware,

That obsession's allure can lead us to despair.

For in its clutches, rationality may wane,

And what we seek may bring only sorrow and pain.

Obsession, a flame that burns too bright, too bold,

May blind us to the treasures we already hold.

Let us find balance, embrace what we adore,

Without succumbing to its alluring lore.

Chandan Malana

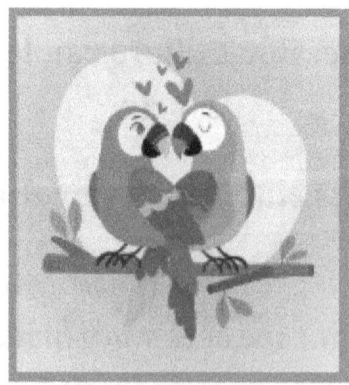

# Quote 10

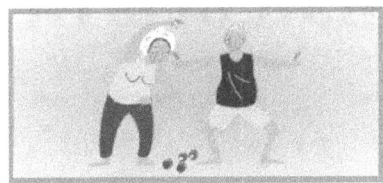

"Obsession's hold is a strange allure,
Even the loveless heart feels insecure.
The fear of losing what we've never
found, Obsession's grip has us
spellbound."

Chandan Malana

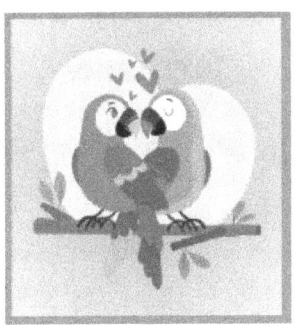

# Fiery Fervor, Unmatched Desire

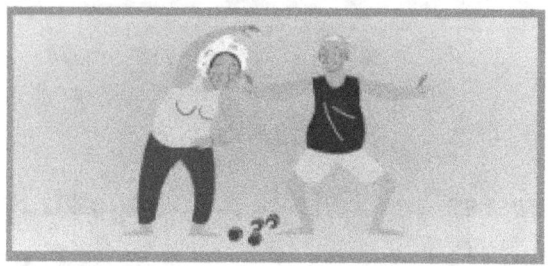

In this game of life, I stand tall and true,

With an unwavering spirit, I conquer and pursue.

For I possess a fire, a winning fortitude,

Guided by love's devotion, my attitude.

Through stormy seas and skies of blue,

I navigate the challenges, as I pursue

A love so profound, it ignites my soul
anew,

Leaving others envious, of the passion I
pursue.



Obsession fuels my every waking hour,

A flame that burns with unyielding
power.

I am consumed by this love so true,

And it's reflected in everything I do.

With every step, my heart beats in
sync,

A melody of desire, a rhythm distinct.

For you, my love, I wear my attitude,

A badge of honor, a testament to
gratitude.

Through every trial, I refuse to yield,

For love's obsession becomes my shield.

With confidence and purpose, I stand
tall,

A devotee of love, ready to give my all.

Envy may swirl around, like a bitter breeze,

But it cannot extinguish the fire that frees.

For in my devotion, I find strength anew,

And in my attitude, I find love that's true.

No obstacle too great, no mountain too high,

With determination, I reach for the sky.

Obsessed with you, my love, I embrace,

An attitude that sets my heart ablaze.

*So let them envy, let them wonder why,*

*For in my love's obsession, I can't deny.*

*I win with attitude, fueled by devotion,*

*A devotee of love, bound by eternal emotion.*

**Chandan Malana**

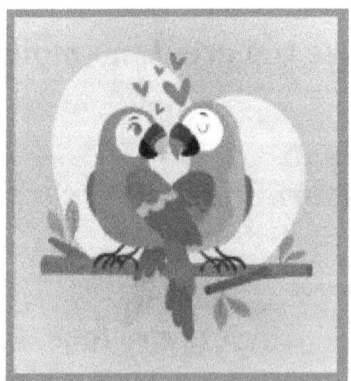

# Quote 11

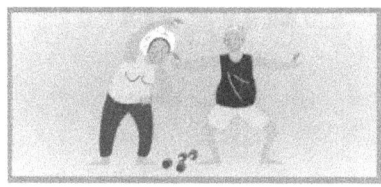

"My love for you fuels my fire, With an attitude that others envy, admire, I've found my devotion, my obsession, my zeal, With you, my love, there's no wound that cannot heal."

Chandan Malana

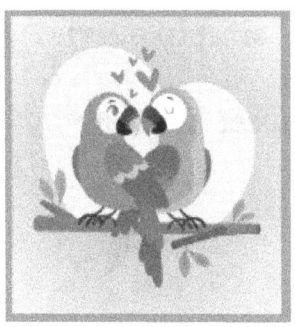

# From Crying To Laughing

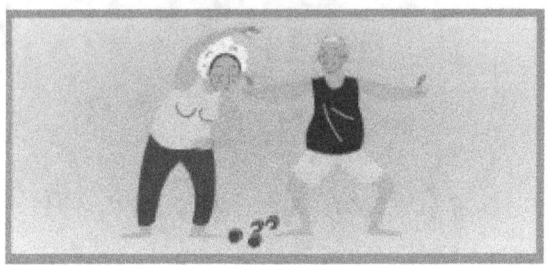

Sometimes crying, sometimes laughing, in love we're dazed,

Emotions intertwine, a wild rollercoaster we ride unfazed,

It grips our hearts, a force we cannot simply outrun,

Love's sweet obsession, a journey begun.

Like a butterfly's dance, it flutters and takes flight,

Through highs and lows, we soar to delight,

Lost in its magic, we dance without fear,

Love's symphony plays, a melody so clear.


In the depths of darkness, it brings a glowing light,

A beacon of hope, a spark shining bright,

When tears stream down like a gentle rain,

Love whispers comfort, easing the pain.

With laughter as its partner, they
waltz as one,

Through joy and euphoria, two souls
are spun,

In a world of chaos, love finds its way,

Guiding us through, come what may.


Obsession takes hold, an enchanting
spell,

In the heart's chambers, it knows so
well,

It paints us crazy, a beautiful haze,

Lost in its rapture, we wander its
maze.

Through seasons of change, love
remains steadfast,

Like roots of a tree, it anchors our past,

Yet, it spreads its wings, sets our
spirits free,

Love's obsession, a boundless decree.


In the quiet moments, when all is still,

Love whispers softly, its essence a
thrill,

Through tears and laughter, it carves
our story,

A tale of devotion, bathed in glory.

So let us embrace this love's grand design,

The tears, the laughter, and feelings divine,

For in its grasp, we find life's true treasure,

Love's obsession, a boundless pleasure.

Chandan Malana

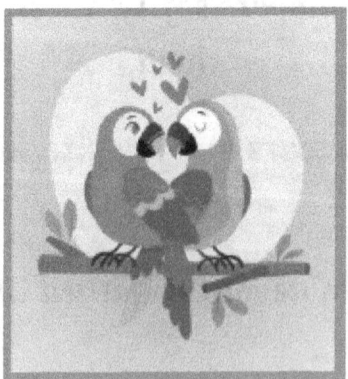

# Quote 12

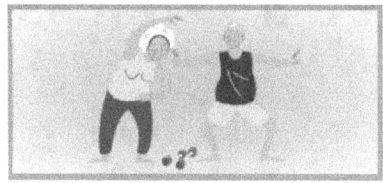

*"Love's emotion is a curious thing, At times tears like rain, at times hearts take wing, Amazement and laughter, or painful despair, The craze of love, a wild and mysterious affair."*

*Chandan Malana*

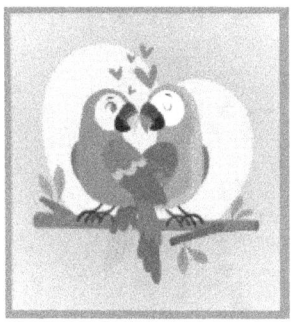

# Heart's Confession, Love's Obsession

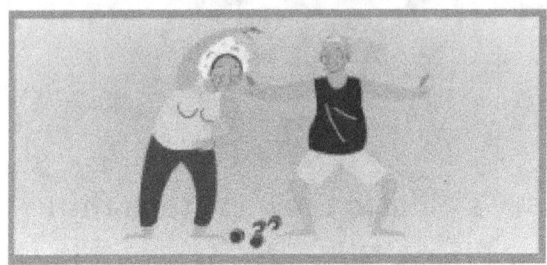

Who dares to claim this heart's
deranged,

Madness a mere guise, it's disdained.

For in a single smile's embrace,

Obsession blooms, consumed by your
grace.

They scoff and jest, blind to the truth,

This fervent love, an eternal sleuth.

No reason nor rhyme can explain,

Why you alone ignite this heart's flame.




With every beat, it yearns for your touch,

An all-consuming need, it craves so much.

No logic can stifle this burning desire,

For you, my love, set this heart on fire.

Oh, doubters, let your doubts be erased,

This madness is not a mere charade.

It's an unwavering devotion, pure and true,

A testament to how much I'm obsessed with you.


In every breath I take, your name resides,

Like a symphony, playing on the tides.

This heart's lunacy knows no end,

Bound to you, forever, my dearest friend.

No asylum can contain this love's spell,

For it's a madness they could never quell.

A madman's plight, a poet's sweetest muse,

In this mad obsession, I find my refuge.


So, let them call this heart insane,

For in their ignorance, they shall remain.

For I've found solace in this obsession,

Where love's madness defies all comprehension.

Who says this heart is crazy, ask they
may,

But this obsession won't waver, come
what may.

For in your presence, my world finds
peace,

This mad heart's obsession will never
cease.

Chandan Malana

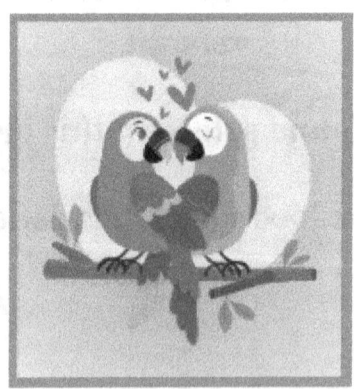

# Quote 13

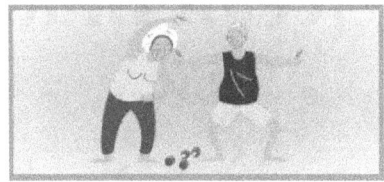

"The world may call it madness, this love that I feel, But a heart that beats for you is nothing but real, So go ahead and smile, let your laughter take flight, For this crazy heart of mine is yours, both day and night."

Chandan Malana

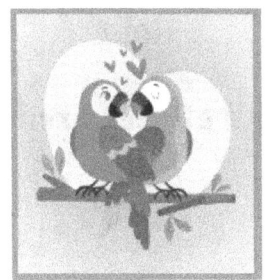

# Hearts' Depths, An Ocean Blue

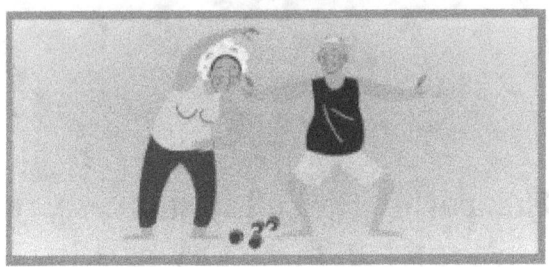

The heart, a vast ocean, deeper than
the sea,

Conceals secrets unknown, a mystic
decree.

Beneath its surface, emotions ebb and
flow,

Obsession's allure, a tempestuous
show.

Who can fathom the depths of this
beating core?

Its desires and yearnings, forever to
explore.

Yet, amidst its mysteries, a truth rings
clear,

A heart's worth is cherished by those
who hold dear.


Give your heart to the one who
understands,

The value of loved ones, the touch of
their hands.

For obsession may blind, a perilous
snare,

But true love's devotion, a treasure
beyond compare.

In passion's grip, hearts may wander
astray,

Lost in the currents that lead hearts
astray.

But a soul aware, in wisdom's embrace,

Will steer love's course with honor and
grace.

Beware the obsession that knows no
release,

For it consumes hearts with relentless
increase.

But a love that is pure, a flame that is
bright,

Will nurture and grow, like stars in the
night.

So guard your heart, like a precious gem,

From obsessions that poison, from feelings condemned.

Seek a love that's genuine, faithful, and true,

Where the depths of your heart find solace anew.


For the heart is a vessel, both fragile and strong,

In its depths, a symphony of emotions belong.

Choose a love that understands, that sets your soul free,

Where the heart's deepest currents find harmony.

The heart, a universe, vast and
untamed,

Yearns for a love that's unconditionally
claimed.

In this realm of emotions, may you
find your way,

To a love that knows value, each and
every day.

**Chandan Malana**

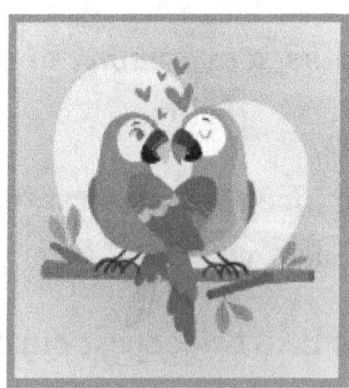

# Quote 14

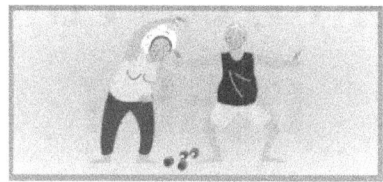

"Amidst the depths of the heart's ocean blue, Lies emotions, secrets, and passions anew, Only the one who cherishes love's essence, Is worthy of the heart's complete quintessence."

Chandan Malana

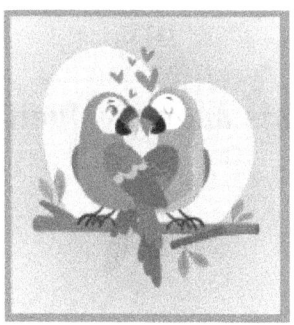

# Heart's Refusal: A Hundred Times Denied

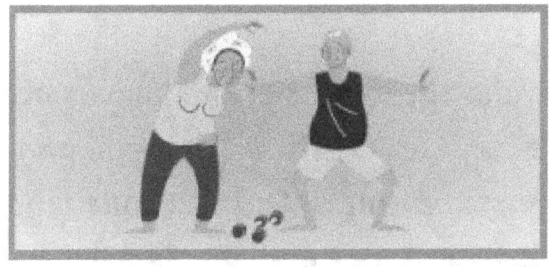

A hundred times I whispered low,

"Let go, release him, let him go."

But my heart, consumed by obsession's fire,

Clung to his memory, fueling desire.

In the depths of longing, I yearned to be free,

From the grip of a love that wouldn't let me flee.

Yet my heart, like a captive, held on tight,

Ignoring reason, embracing the night.


A hundred times I pleaded, "Set me free,

From this web of emotions that torment me."

But my heart, stubborn and resolute,

Clung to the dreams it refused to refute.

In the battle of heart versus mind,

Love's stronghold prevailed, leaving
reason behind.

A hundred times I tried to explain,

Yet my heart remained steadfast,
causing me pain.

The words from my lips fell on deaf
ears,

As my heart held tight to its cherished
fears.

A hundred times, in anguish, I cried,

But my heart, relentless, would not be
denied.

With each passing day, the ache grew
strong,

An unyielding obsession that felt so
wrong.

A hundred times I sought an escape,

But my heart's grip tightened, like a
lover's cape.


Oh, the torment of love's relentless
hold,

As my heart refused to do as it was
told.

A hundred times, I pleaded, begged,
and implored,

Yet my heart, like a prisoner, stayed
aboard.

*In the depths of my soul, I longed for release,*

*From the clutches of a love that wouldn't cease.*

*A hundred times, I said from the heart,*

*"Go on, forget him too." But we never truly part.*

**Chandan Malana**

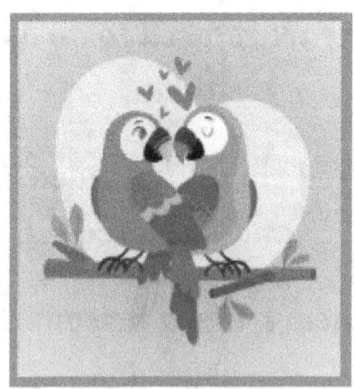

# Quote 15

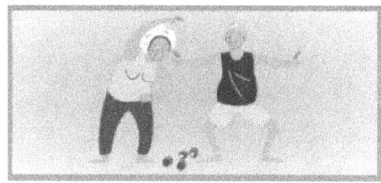

"From deep within, a hundred times I tried, To say, "move on," my heart I did chide, "But you don't mean it," my heart replied, In a battle of wills with my heart, I couldn't decide."

Chandan Malana

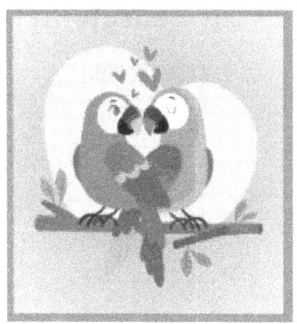

# Her Beauty Struck

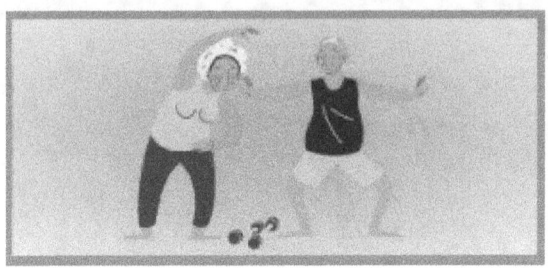

Once I caught sight of her, my heart
went ablaze,

Her beauty so captivating, in a
thousand ways.

I was consumed by a fire, a burning
desire,

To unravel the secrets her eyes did
inspire.

Her presence alone, a magnetic force,

I was enchanted, lost in a wild
discourse.

Every moment without her, an eternity
of pain,

Her image etched in my mind, driving
me insane.

Her smile, like sunshine on a cloudy
day,

It illuminated my world in an
enchanting display.

Her laughter, a symphony that danced
in the air,

I yearned to be near her, to show her I
care.

Her voice, a melody that echoed in my soul,

Each word she spoke, like a spell to behold.

I was captivated, intoxicated by her spell,

Her essence consumed me, in a love's dwell.


Her touch, a feather grazing my skin,

Sending shivers down my spine, from deep within.

I longed for her embrace, to hold her tight,

To be lost in her arms, throughout the night.

Her scent, like a fragrant blossom in bloom,

It filled the air, enveloping every room.

I breathed it in, intoxicated by her perfume,

Her presence lingering, even in the empty gloom.


Her grace, like a dancer on a moonlit stage,

Her movements so fluid, captivating in every gauge.

I watched in awe, unable to tear my eyes away,

Her elegance and charm leaving me in disarray.

*Once I saw her, she made me go crazy,*

*In her presence, I felt both weak and hazy.*

*Obsession took hold, and I couldn't break free,*

*For she had become the sole obsession of me.*

**Chandan Malana**

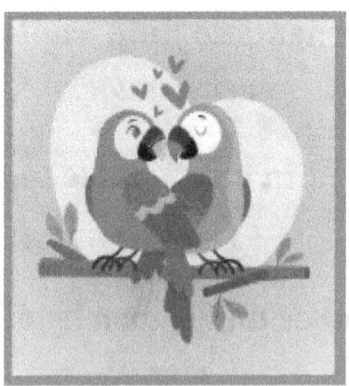

# Quote 16

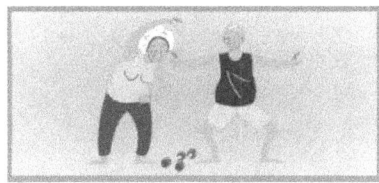

"With just one glance, my heart ablaze,
Her captivating beauty, set me in a
daze, I was powerless, lost in her eyes
so blue, Nothing else mattered, the
world faded from view."

Chandan Malana

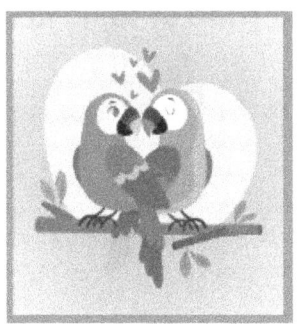

# Her Toyed Heart

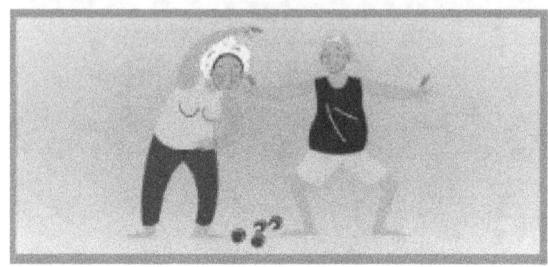

She danced upon my heart's delicate strings,

Her touch, a symphony that made me sing,

But little did I know, her game was cruel,

A masquerade of love, her heart a jewel.

She toyed with my emotions, like a puppeteer,

Each tug of her strings, bringing me near,

I surrendered my soul, so willingly,

Unaware of the trap she set for me.

In her hands, my love became a game,

She reveled in my agony, without shame,

Her laughter echoed, mocking my affection,

As I drowned in the depths of my obsession.

Her smiles were daggers, piercing my
soul,

While I yearned for her touch, to make
me whole,

But she danced away, leaving me in
despair,

A broken heart, consumed by love's
snare.


I tried to break free, to escape her spell,

But her enchantment held me, too
strong to quell,

Her siren's song, a haunting melody,

Keeping me captive in her web of glee.

Oh, how I longed for her love's sweet
embrace,

But she played with my heart, leaving
no trace,

Her whims a storm, tearing me apart,

Yet I remained devoted, foolishly
smitten from the start.


Now I stand here, a mere shell of my
past,

Haunted by memories that forever will
last,

She played with my love, a master of
deception,

Leaving me with wounds, a lasting
impression.

But I'll rise from the ashes, a phoenix anew,

For love's bitter lessons have made me true,

No longer a victim of her cruel game,

I'll find a love that's worthy of my flame.

**Chandan Malana**

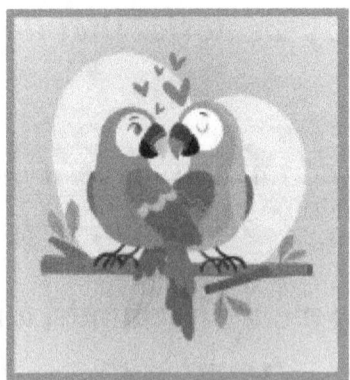

# Quote 17

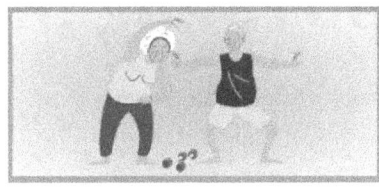

"She toyed with fire, my heart in her hand, A dangerous game, a love that's grand. I burned with desire, consumed by her touch, While she laughed and played, her heart cold as such."

Chandan Malana

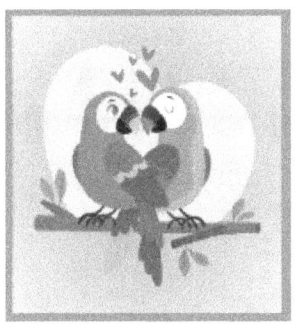

# Her Words' Captivating Sting

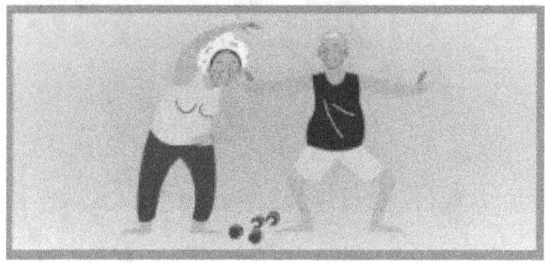

She whispered softly, like a velvet breeze,

Her words entwined my thoughts, brought me to my knees.

With every syllable, my heart would race,

Her mere presence enough to set my world ablaze.

Her voice, a symphony that played in my mind,

A melody so sweet, impossible to find.

Each word she spoke, a spell she cast,

A potion of obsession, too potent to outlast.


Her sentences danced, graceful and sublime,

Enchanting my senses, freezing the hands of time.

Every phrase she uttered, a poetic verse,

Her linguistic prowess, a curse I couldn't reverse.

Her language, a weapon, cutting
through the air,

Leaving me breathless, consumed by
her glare.

Each sentence, a puzzle I yearned to
decode,

A riddle of passion, with her as the ode.



Her whispers echoed, resonating deep
within,

A spellbinding chant, a spell I couldn't
rescind.

Her words, like tendrils, wrapped
around my core,

Leaving me craving, always wanting
more.

She spoke in riddles, secrets in her tone,

Unlocking desires I never knew I'd known.

Her voice, a siren's call, irresistible and fierce,

Tying my emotions, leaving me immersed.


Her phrases haunted, lingering in my mind,

A fixation I couldn't leave behind.

Her linguistic sorcery, a dangerous game,

Leaving me entangled, forever under her name.

She held the power, with just a few words,

A bewitching enchantress, setting my soul ablaze.

Without confessing love, she drove me insane,

Obsession consumed me, and I was forever her slave.

Chandan Malana

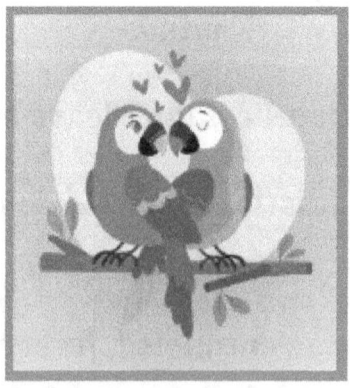

# Quote 18

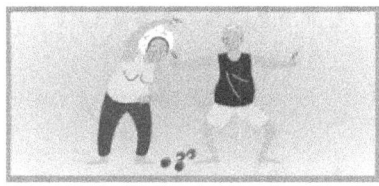

*"Her words struck a match, set my heart ablaze, My mind was captured in a passionate daze. Lost in her spell, consumed by her charm, A love unspoken, in my heart, did form."*

## Chandan Malana

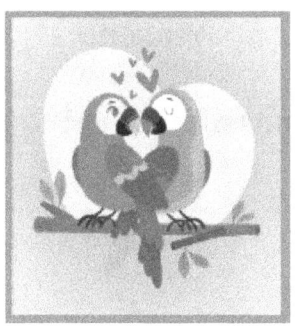

# Love Turns To Obsession

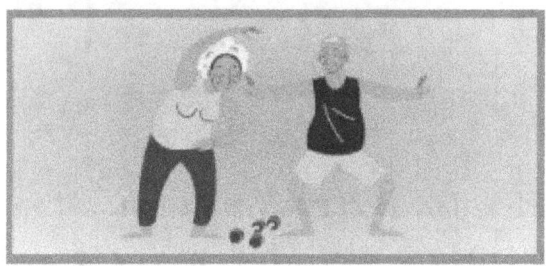

Love, once pure and gentle, now transformed,

Obsession takes hold, its flames adorned.

Ecstatic, it dances, consuming all reason,

A fiery passion, burning in every season.

No joy can temper, nor sorrow can
break,

In its grip, the heart and soul do
partake.

Unfazed by the trials that life may
bring,

Obsession's power, an unyielding sting.

It clings to the heart with a fervent
embrace,

Leaving no room for doubt or a
moment's space.

A whirlwind of desire, a relentless tide,

Love turned obsession, impossible to
hide.

In its depths, one finds a dangerous
allure,

A tempestuous flame that burns ever
pure.

The mind consumed, thoughts centered
on one,

Obsession's grip, a battle never won.




Like a moth drawn to a mesmerizing
light,

Love's transformation, an endless fight.

Ecstasy and agony, entwined hand in
hand,

Obsession's hold, a relentless demand.

Through passion's haze, reason fades
away,

Love's boundaries blurred; colors turn
gray.

Unyielding devotion, a thirst never
quenched,

Obsession's allure, forever entrenched.


Yet, amidst the chaos and consuming
fire,

A glimmer of hope, a chance to inspire.

To recognize the boundaries love
should keep,

And reclaim a love that's pure, not
steeped.

*For love turned obsession, though powerful and grand,*

*Must find its balance to truly withstand.*

*In the delicate dance of heart and mind's reflection,*

*Love can transcend obsession, finding true affection.*

**Chandan Malana**

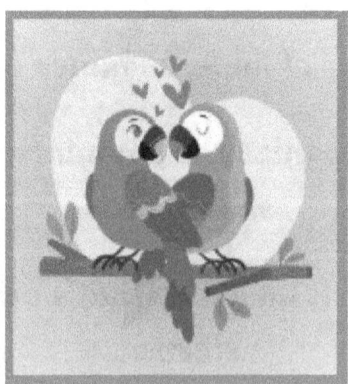

# Quote 19

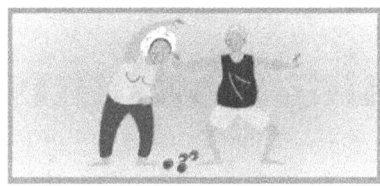

"As love turns to obsession, emotions soar, Ecstasy reigns, and every moment is pure, Joy or sorrow, nothing can ever obscure, Our passion for each other, so enduring and secure."

Chandan Malana

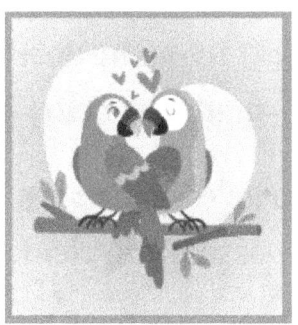

# Love's Definition: Beyond Possession, A Feeling's Submission

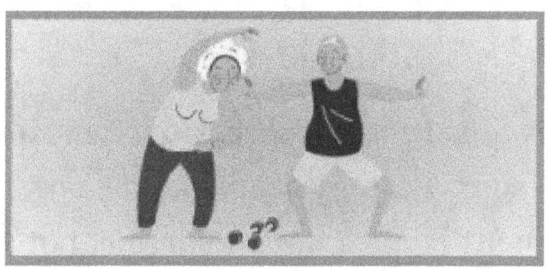

There is no excuse for loving someone dear,

With hearts entwined, passion may appear.

But mere attachment does not bring madness near,

Love's true essence goes beyond possession, clear.

To understand love, one must delve deep,

It's not a game where possession you keep.

Obsession blinds, causing hearts to weep,

True love's selfless nature, in its secrets we reap.


In love's vast garden, emotions bloom,

But beware of obsession's dark gloom.

For it twists the heart, causing endless doom,

Love's purest form, a sacred heirloom.

Let love be gentle, like a summer
breeze,

Not a raging storm that brings unease.

Obsession's chains, love must release,

In freedom's embrace, love finds its
peace.


Love is not a contest, where winners
claim,

Nor a possession to play, like a
dangerous game.

Obsession's flames ignite, leaving
hearts in shame,

Love's true power lies in setting hearts
aflame.

Embrace love's beauty with an open
heart,

But guard against obsession tearing
love apart.

For love is freedom, a precious work of
art,

In its gentle dance, souls never depart.

So let us love, with grace and care,

Knowing that obsession is not love's
fair.

Love is understanding, a bond we
share,

A priceless gift, beyond compare.

No excuse exists for loving's sweet desire,

For love is pure, it sets our souls afire.

Let go of possession, let love inspire,

In its boundless depths, our spirits aspire.

**Chandan Malana**

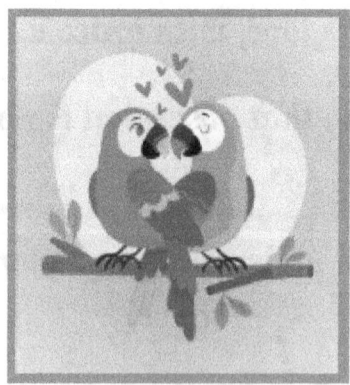

# Quote 20

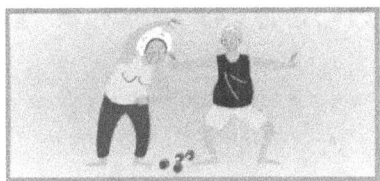

"Love isn't a mere possession to hold,
One can't just attach and hope to
behold, It's about giving, sharing, and
caring with dedication, Not an excuse,
but a feeling beyond explanation."

Chandan Malana

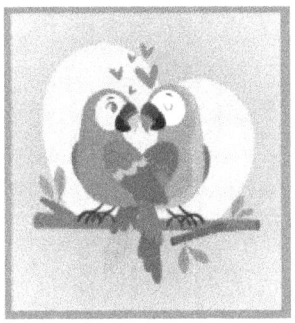

# Love's Snare, Obsession's Flare

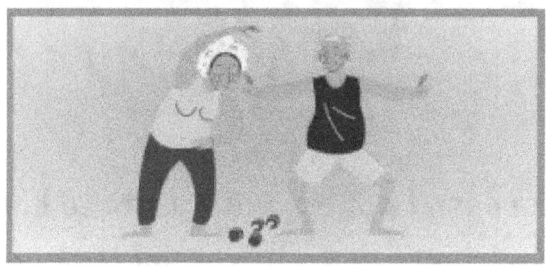

Love's tangled web, a tempting snare,

Obsession's grip, I can't repair.

Bound by desire, in these confines,

Lost in the maze of intertwining lines.

Oh, how I yearn, with a heavy heart,

To break free from this love's wicked art.

Yet I find solace in your tender embrace,

A bittersweet refuge, a fleeting grace.

In your eyes, I see my reflection,

A mirror of love, a dangerous affection.

Ensnared in the depths of your captivating spell,

I surrender my soul, to heaven or to hell.

Every breath I take, a desperate plea,

To be consumed by your love's decree.

In this twisted dance, I am both captor
and prey,

Trapped in the rhythm, night and day.


The chains that bind, they tighten
their hold,

Yet I crave the warmth, the stories
untold.

Whispers of passion, secrets concealed,

In this tangled web, my fate is sealed.

But still, I hope for a glimpse of light,

For love's true essence to come into
sight.

To find in your heart a sanctuary of
peace,

Where my restless soul can finally find
release.


Yet, even in this trap, I cannot deny,

The ecstasy found in your gaze, oh,
how high!

For love, though it binds, also sets me
free,

A paradoxical prison where I long to
be.

So I surrender to the allure of your
name,

In this labyrinth of love, I bear no
shame.

For love is a trap, obsession's chains,

Yet in your embrace, my heart
remains.


Chandan Malana

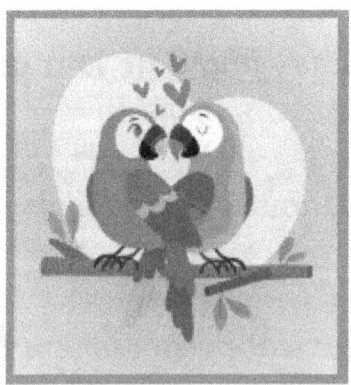

# Quote 21

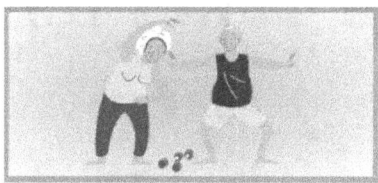

"Love is a trap and obsession's chains, I love you deeply with endless pains, My fate is tied to what comes next, I hope in your heart I will find rest."

Chandan Malana

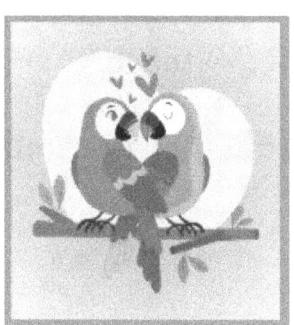

# Manipulation's Hold Takes Its Toll

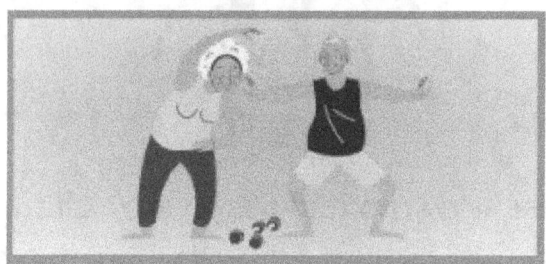

To *weave a web of passion's fire,*

To *captivate their heart's desire,*

With *whispered words and gentle touch,*

In *admiration they are smitten much.*

But in this game of love and chase,

Deception finds its hiding place,

For promises made, now empty air,

Leaving hearts in disrepair.


In anger's grip, we lose control,

Claiming helplessness, breaking the
whole,

A relationship once vibrant and grand,

Falls apart like grains of sand.

Is this the love we claim to know?

An obsession that's destined to sow,

False vows and promises untrue,

Leaving souls adrift and blue.


We yearn for love, a devotion deep,

Yet shallow waters are all we reap,

Turning sour, bidding farewell,

In the aftermath, love's bitter spell.

But let us question, if we may,

Is this the essence we long to portray?

An obsession born from fleeting lust,

Leaving hearts crumbled, lost and thrust.


To make someone a devoted thrall,

Is not the truest love of all,

For love should lift and inspire,

Not drown in deceit's mire.

Let us seek love's pure embrace,

A connection built on truth and grace,

Where promises are steadfast and
strong,

And hearts sing a harmonious song.

Chandan Malana

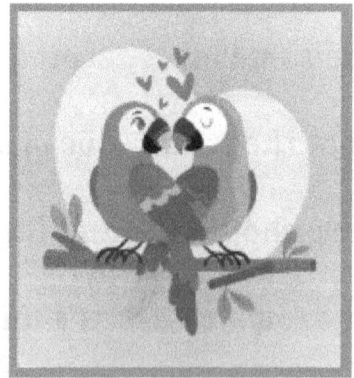

# Quote 22

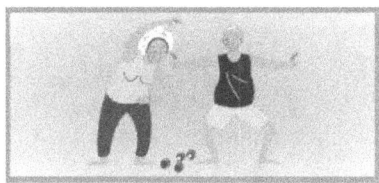

*"Love isn't just a tool for manipulation, Nor a game to play with hearts in animation, It's about honesty, respect, and devotion, Not a means to gain control with cunning commotion."*

Chandan Malana

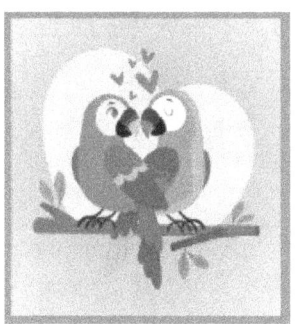

# Miraculous Feeling

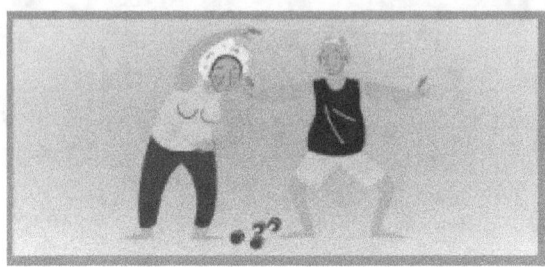

Sometimes I weep, tears streaming down my face,

Lost in a sorrowful, melancholic embrace,

But then laughter bursts forth, like a symphony,

Filling my soul with joy, setting me free.

Moments of awe, when I stand in disbelief,

Witnessing miracles, beyond my own belief,

Amazed and astounded by life's grand design,

In every corner, a masterpiece to find.


Love, a force that defies all logic and reason,

Transforms the ordinary into a vibrant season,

With passion's flame, it sets my heart ablaze,

An obsession that guides me through life's maze.

In tears, I find solace, release, and
relief,

A healing balm, easing my heart's deep
grief,

Yet laughter uplifts me, with its joyous
might,

A symphony of mirth, bringing
warmth to the night.


Astounded by beauty, nature's
breathtaking art,

Stars sprinkled across the canvas, a
celestial chart,

In wonder, I stand, humbled by the vast
expanse,

Immersed in a universe, where
miracles enhance.

Love, the essence that turns the
ordinary insane,

A power that captivates, dances within
every vein,

Obsession takes hold, in its enchanting
sway,

Guiding my steps, with passion's
fervent display.


Through tears and laughter, I find my
truest self,

Embracing the highs and lows, like a
book on a shelf,

For in the duality of life's emotions, I'm
set free,

Discovering the beauty of being both
you and me.

So let the tears flow and the laughter resound,

In awe and in love, let our hearts be unbound,

For it's in the depths of our emotions we find,

The richness of existence, intertwined.

Chandan Malana

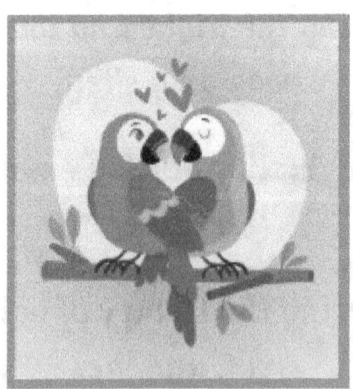

# Quote 23

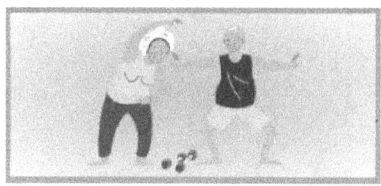

*"Love can bring tears or make us laugh, It can fill us with wonder, even on a darkened path, Making even the mundane seem insane, Such is the power of love's unstoppable reign."*

Chandan Malana

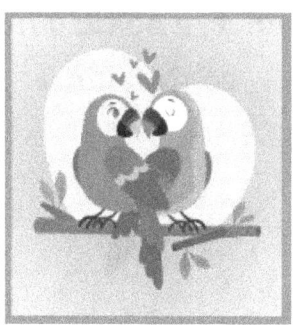

# No Excuses Needed

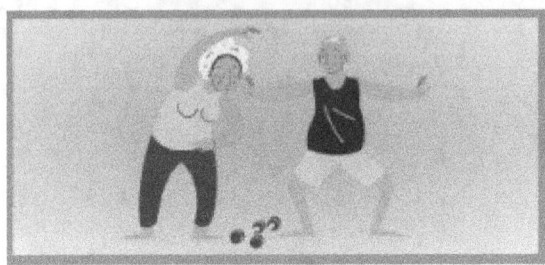

There is no excuse to love someone,

A force that binds, like the morning
sun.

Yet love is not an excuse for possession,

It's a choice, a bond, a heartfelt
confession.

No one becomes Obsession just by
falling in love,

For love is gentle, like a cooing dove.

Obsession stems from a darker place,

Where boundaries blur and hearts give
chase.


If you want to learn true love's sweet
art,

Open your soul, let it mend and
restart.

For love is patient, it's kind and serene,

It's a symphony of hearts, a sacred
dream.

Know that we cannot find the meaning
of love,

In dictionaries or books written above.

Love is felt in whispers, in tender
caress,

It's a language unspoken, a silent
address.


So let love blossom, like flowers in
bloom,

In hearts intertwined, dispelling all
gloom.

For love knows no boundaries, no walls
or divide,

It's a tapestry of emotions, where souls
confide.

In love, there's forgiveness, a chance to heal,

A refuge of solace, where wounds can seal.

But obsession consumes, it devours and takes,

Leaving emptiness, hearts shattered in its wake.


True love is freedom, it gives wings to fly,

It celebrates uniqueness, it never asks why.

But obsession seeks control, it smothers and binds,

Leaving no room for growth, no space for minds.

So cherish true love, let it guide your way,

In its gentle embrace, find peace every day.

For love is a gift, a precious, divine treasure,

A journey of souls, beyond measure.

Chandan Malana

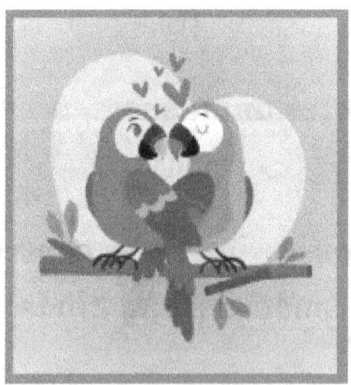

# Quote 24

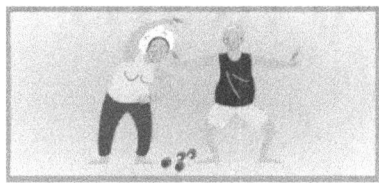

"With love, there is no excuse to be found, For obsession is not where it is bound, In true love, no control can be found, For its meaning cannot be unwound."

Chandan Malana

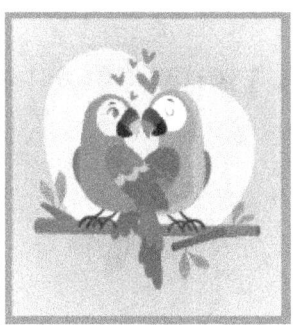

# No Sin In Love: When Hearts Afire

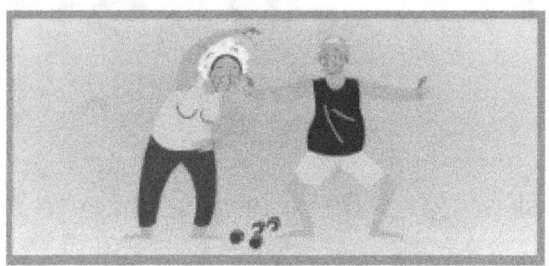

If love's obsession claims the heart,

A passion fierce, a fiery start,

No sin it is, but fate's decree,

For love, a force that sets us free.

In mad desire, emotions soar,

A torrential wave forevermore,

Bound by love's intoxicating spell,

In its embrace, we dance and dwell.


No mortal hand did forge this flame,

Divine intervention, the only name,

For love, an enchantment from above,

A gift bestowed, a celestial dove.

In love's madness, reason may depart,

But who can quell the beating heart?

When souls entwined in a fervent
dance,

The world dissolves, and time's mere
chance.


A mad devotion, all-consuming fire,

A craving deep, a never-ending desire,

In love's embrace, we find our peace,

Where passion's flames can never
cease.

Though others may deem it a sin to behold,

Love's madness, an enigma untold,

The heart's dictation, beyond control,

Unraveling mysteries, hidden in soul.


In mad love's grip, we surrender all,

Breaking barriers, scaling the wall,

For love, a force that defies all reason,

It knows no bounds, nor any season.

So let us revel in love's divine sin,

Where hearts entwined, a symphony begins,

For madly in love, we find our true bliss,

A testament to the magic of Cupid's kiss.

Chandan Malana

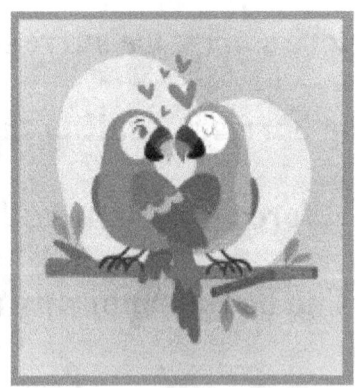

# Quote 25

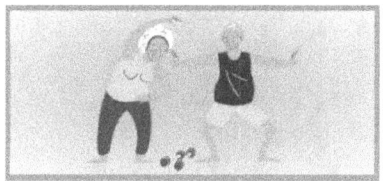

"When love takes hold, it's beyond our control, Divine intervention, a higher power's role, No sin in loving, just let your heart unroll, A beautiful journey, together you can stroll."

Chandan Malana

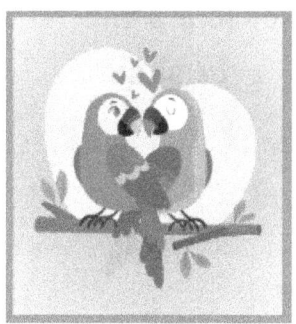

# Obsessed Man

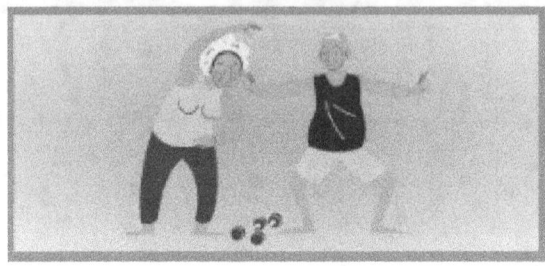

In the realm of the obsessed, hearts stray,

No dwelling they crave, nor walls to call their own.

Their souls entwined in passion's fervent play,

Yearning for love's gaze, a warmth to be shown.

Like a moth drawn to a flame's
hypnotic light,

Obsession consumes, no logic can
contain.

They forsake the comfort of a sheltered
night,

Seeking instead love's embrace, its
sweet refrain.

Their minds consumed by one sole
desire,

A fixated obsession, a relentless chase.

No earthly abode can quench their
inner fire,

Only love's glance can fill the empty
space.

They wander lost, driven by their own
devotion,

No hearth or haven can satiate their
thirst.

For them, love's gaze is the ultimate
potion,

A treasure sought, an eternal love
cursed.




In their eyes, a hunger that knows no
end,

An insatiable need for affection's bliss.

The obsession consumes, they cannot
pretend,

A home is forsaken for love's gentle
kiss.

They dance through life, fueled by their infatuation,

Unburdened by the weight of worldly ties.

No four walls can hold their wild elation,

Only love's gaze can grant the solace they prize.


A nomadic existence, their hearts ever roaming,

In search of the love that will make them whole.

Their obsession, a force that keeps them from homing,

Yet within love's gaze, they find their truest role.

So let them wander, these obsessed
souls,

For they are driven by an unearthly
force.

In love's gaze, they find their ultimate
goal,

No dwelling they need, only love's
fierce course.

Chandan Malana

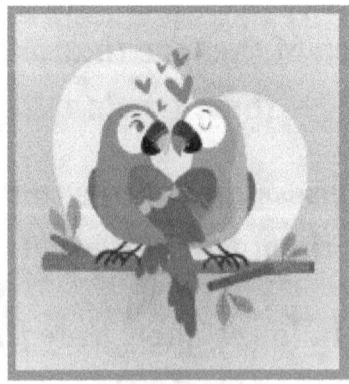

# Quote 26

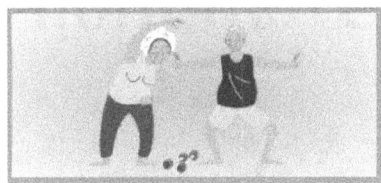

"Driven by love, consumed by passion,
No need for home, just a lover's
attraction. The obsessed man's heart
beats with desire, A heavy glance of
love, the only fire."

Chandan Malana

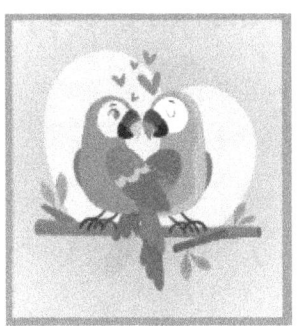

# Obsession's Definition

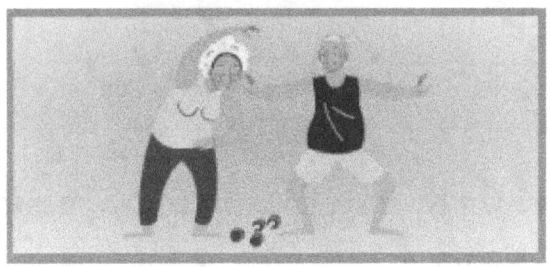

*In the realm of hearts, a fire is ablaze,*

*Obsession's grip, an intricate maze.*

*I am the word, weaving desires unbound,*

*You are the meaning, the purpose I've found.*

Without you, existence is an empty
shell,

Obsession's currents, where my soul
dwells.

In every breath, your essence takes
flight,

A relentless yearning, day and night.

Through tangled thoughts, my mind
does roam,

Obsession's seeds, firmly sown.

You are the compass, guiding my way,

Lost in your essence, I long to stay.

With every heartbeat, your presence
persists,

Obsession's flame, never ceasing to
persist.

I am the vessel, consumed by your
might,

Enthralled by your aura, my guiding
light.

A fevered devotion, in every heartbeat,

Obsession's dance, with passions so
sweet.

Bound by desire, an unyielding
embrace,

You are the epitome of love's fierce
grace.

*In dreams I wander, where fantasies
unfold,*

*Obsession's whispers, secrets untold.*

*You are the rhythm, in each verse I
recite,*

*A symphony of longing, burning bright.*

*In your absence, emptiness takes hold,*

*Obsession's void, a story untold.*

*I am the poet, forever in your sway,*

*Drunk on your essence, night and day.*

Obsession's definition, an endless chase,

I am the word, forever in your embrace.

You are the meaning, the reason I'm alive,

Obsession's ardor, my soul's eternal drive.


Chandan Malana

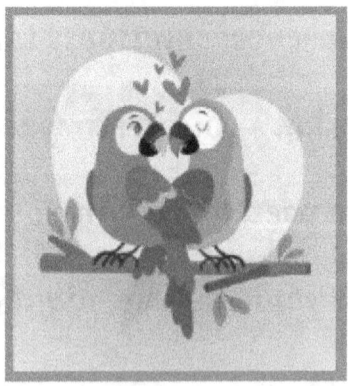

# Quote 27

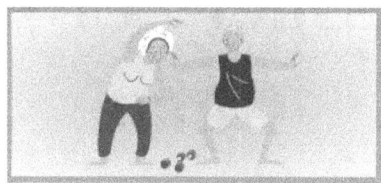

"Obsession, a state beyond reason and sense, Where I'm the word, and you're the essence, Without you, life would be a hollow pretense, For obsession makes every other meaning less dense."

Chandan Malana

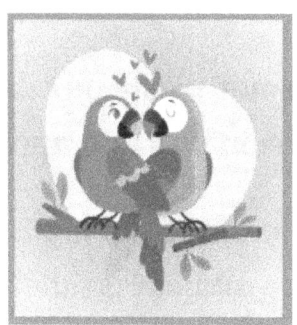

# Obsession's Flame: A Short-Lived Game

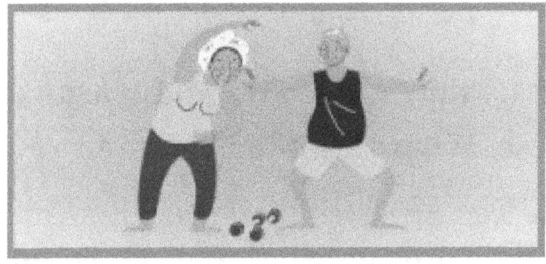

Life is too short, a fleeting breath we
borrow,

May it not pass in strife, in conflict
and sorrow.

Let us not waste our days in
disagreements and apologies,

Instead, embrace the moments with
love and camaraderie.

Our time on Earth is limited, it swiftly
slips away,

So let us not be consumed by
obsession's sway.

For in pursuit of material desires, we
may lose sight,

Of the simple joys and treasures that
make life bright.


May our hearts be free from the chains
of obsession's hold,

That binds us in a quest to make you
fit a mold.

Let us embrace acceptance,
understanding, and grace,

And cherish the diversity that each
soul does embrace.

Life's canvas is painted with colors
vast and grand,

May it not pass in trying to make you
understand.

Instead, let us listen, with open hearts
and ears,

To the stories and perspectives that
dissolve our fears.


Life's tapestry weaves a complex and
intricate design,

May it not pass in trying to explain
this alone, resign.

For together, we can unravel life's
mysteries and woe,

Supporting one another as we learn
and grow.

In the blink of an eye, the years swiftly
go by,

May we not let precious moments slip
us by.

Let us savor every laughter, every
touch, and smile,

For these are the moments that make
life worthwhile.


Life is too short to dwell on past
mistakes and regret,

May we find forgiveness and move
forward, never forget.

Let us cherish the present, for it is a
precious gift,

And create memories that our souls
will forever uplift.

*So let us embrace the brevity of life's fleeting spark,*

*May it not pass in darkness, but in a radiant arc.*

*With gratitude and love, let us seize each passing day,*

*For life is too short to waste, let's make the most of our stay.*

Chandan Malana

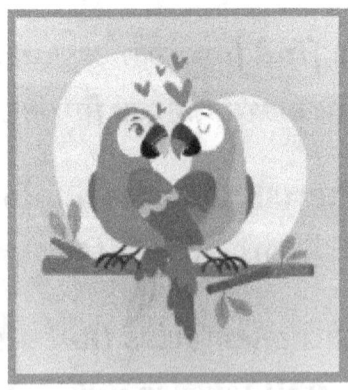

# Quote 28

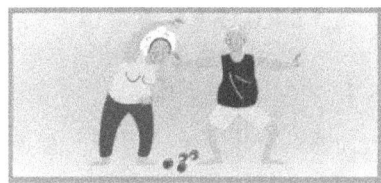

*"Let us not dwell in the darkness of strife, But embrace the light of love in our life, Our passion for you, an obsession true, Let it not wane, in apologies or rue."*

Chandan Malana

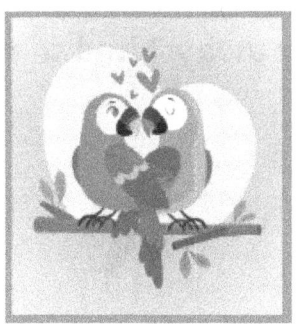

# Obsession's Hold,
# In Silence Bold

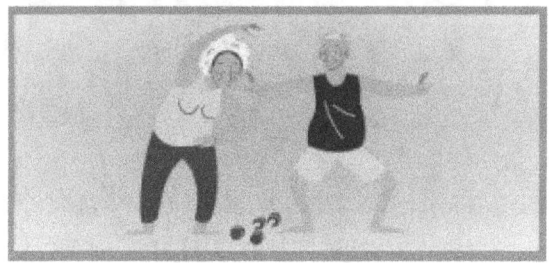

*Some people, lost in their own
thoughts,*

*Fail to inquire how my heart fought,*

*In this labyrinth of obsession's might,*

*They turn away, blind to my plight.*

A whirlwind of madness consumes my
mind,

Yet they remain indifferent, so unkind,

They shy away from the poetry I speak,

A flame within, they refuse to seek.


But I shall recreate, from depths
unknown,

My verses shall bloom, like seeds long
sown,

For my obsession, a flame that burns
bright,

Shall illuminate the darkness of their
sight.

I rhyme with passion, with fervent
desire,

As my words flow, like a raging fire,

They may turn a deaf ear, a blind eye,

But my poetry will soar, reaching the
sky.

Obsession may label me a crazy soul,

But it fuels my spirit, makes me whole,

I'll spin tales of love, of anguish, of
pain,

And leave them wondering, what they
could gain.

For those who don't listen, who don't believe,

They'll miss the magic, the stories I weave,

But I'll keep writing, undeterred by their scorn,

For in my obsession, a new world is born.


Let them judge, let them dismiss my art,

For deep within, it ignites my heart,

With every word, a piece of me unfurled,

Obsession drives me to reshape the world.

*So even if they turn away, never ask,*

*I'll continue to write, fulfill my task,*

*For poetry is my solace, my saving grace,*

*And in its embrace, I find my rightful place.*

**Chandan Malana**

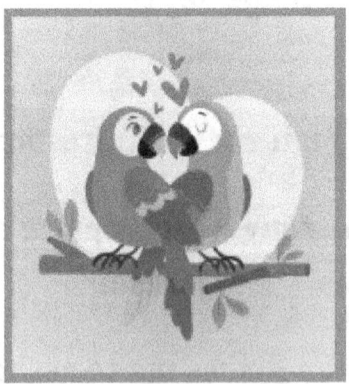

# Quote 29

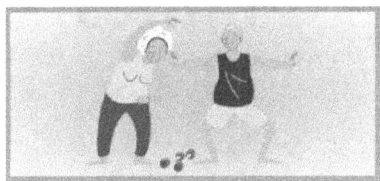

"Their silence speaks volumes, a stark divide, As obsession's flames within me wildly abide, But I will not let their lack of care, Diminish the passion that I endlessly bear."

*Chandan Malana*

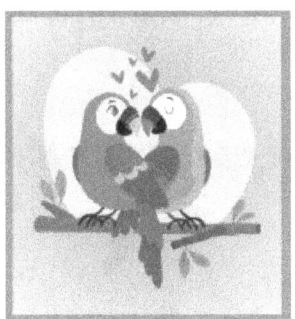

# Old Habits, New Flames

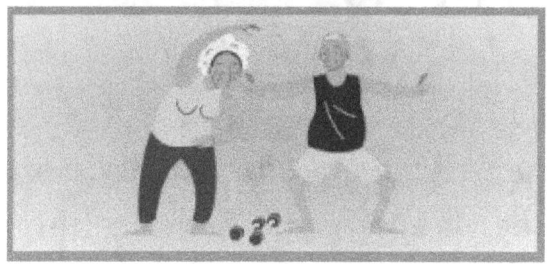

To steal my heart, with glimmer in their gaze,

Your eyes possess ancient, captivating ways.

They beckon and allure, an age-old habit,

Drawing me closer, with their hypnotic orbit.

Stealing my heart, they dance with a
spell,

Like ancient thieves, in secrets they
dwell.

Their allure, unyielding, refuses to
fade,

Ensnaring my soul in a passionate
cascade.


In their depths, a tale unfolds with
grace,

Our obsession, a saga that time can't
erase.

Each stolen glance, a chapter in our
book,

Bound by desire, with a longing that
shook.

Those eyes, like ancient treasures of
lore,

Hold secrets and mysteries,
forevermore.

They whisper of a love that transcends
all,

An obsession that binds us, never to
fall.


Through stolen moments, our story
unfolds,

A tapestry woven with desires untold.

Your eyes, my weakness, my soul's
great lure,

A timeless obsession, steadfast and
pure.

In their depths, I find solace and peace,

A sanctuary where passion will never
cease.

With every stolen beat, my heart they
claim,

Bound to your gaze, forever the same.


Oh, those eyes, a portal to another
realm,

Stealing my heart, like a sacred helm.

Our obsession, a flame that will forever
burn,

A love so intense, it's impossible to
discern.

So let them steal, these eyes of old habit,

For in their theft, a love we cannot forfeit.

Our obsession, a melody that will forever play,

In the depths of our hearts, until the end of days.

Chandan Malana

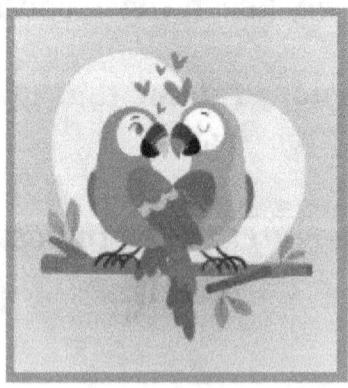

# Quote 30

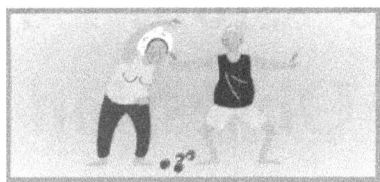

*"Your piercing gaze cuts through the night, Stealing my heart with its ancient might, And as our obsession starts to ignite, Our love's tale takes hold and takes flight."*

## Chandan Malana

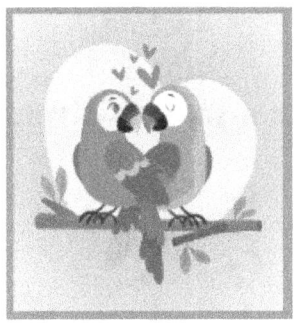

# Pain And Possession: Love's Obsession

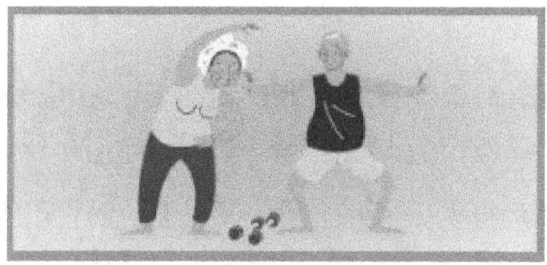

Where will you seek a soul so rare,

An Obsession man with love to share?

Through winding paths and realms
untold,

A heart like mine, yet strong and bold.

In moonlit forests, whispers deep,

Where shadows dance, secrets to keep.

Amongst the stars, where dreams
reside,

There, my love, you may find your
guide.


Through ancient tomes of forgotten
lore,

In dusty pages, my essence pours.

A yearning flame, forever ablaze,

Within those words, my heart displays.

Upon the ocean's endless tide,

Where waves caress and fears subside.

In depths unknown, my passion
thrives,

Where souls converge, true love
survives.


In echoes of a haunting melody,

Through notes that carry, boundlessly.

In music's grasp, my spirit dwells,

Where symphonies of love compel.

Within the hues of a painter's stroke,

Where vibrant colors evoke and evoke.

On canvas vast, my essence blooms,

Where artistry and obsession
entwines.


In whispered prayers, on bended knee,

Where faith and devotion intertwine
free.

In sacred spaces, my soul does roam,

Where love's devotion finds its home.

But seek not far, for here I stand,

An Obsession man, with outstretched hand.

Through joys and sorrows, I'll love you true,

Forever entwined, my heart with you.

Chandan Malana

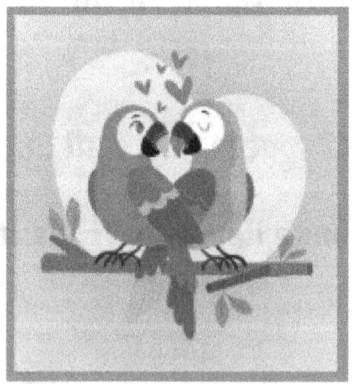

# Quote 31

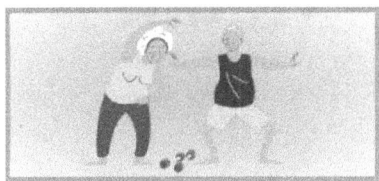

*"In the depths of devotion's sacred shrine, Where souls intertwine and hearts align, A rare Obsession man, I'll surely be found, Enduring sorrows, with love unbound."*

**Chandan Malana**

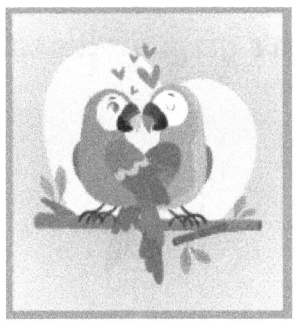

# Paradox Of Madness

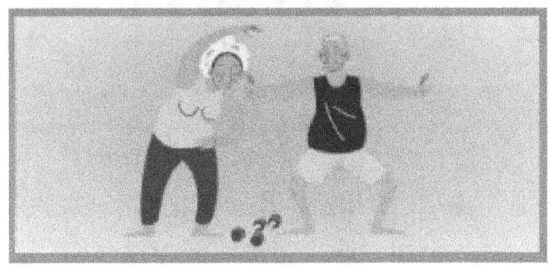

They scoff and sneer, with words
unkind,

But in our hearts, a fire they'll find,

For in our minds, a flame does burn,

Obsession's grip, we'll never spurn.

Through sleepless nights and restless days,

We chase our dreams in countless ways,

The world may deem us lost and strange,

But in our madness, worlds we'll change.


In art and science, love and song,

Obsession drives us to push along,

We dive into depths, explore the unknown,

For passion's seed in us is sown.

They call us mad, yet fail to see,

The beauty born from insanity,

For it's the mad who dare to dream,

And paint reality with colors supreme.


In every stroke of the artist's brush,

In every word, the poet's hush,

Obsession fuels the creative fire,

And lifts our souls to heights much
higher.

The mad are bound by invisible chains,

But through obsession, we break those reins,

We dance with madness, hand in hand,

And leave our mark upon the land.


So let them mock and let them jeer,

For we, the mad, have nothing to fear,

In our obsession, we find our might,

And shape a world that's bold and bright.

For who is truly sane or mad?

In this vast universe we've had,

We all possess a touch of the flame,

Obsession's legacy, forever the same.

Chandan Malana

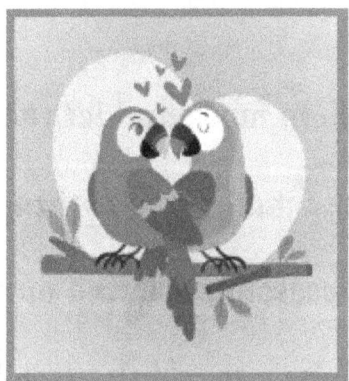

# Quote 32

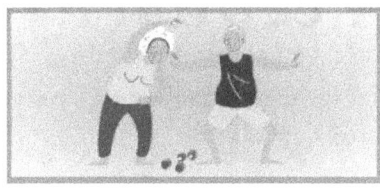

*"In the eyes of the sane, we are but mad, Yet they fail to see the passion we've had, For who can explain the fire inside, Obsession and passion, an unbreakable tide."*

Chandan Malana

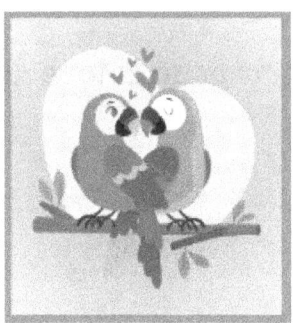

# Passion's Peculiarity

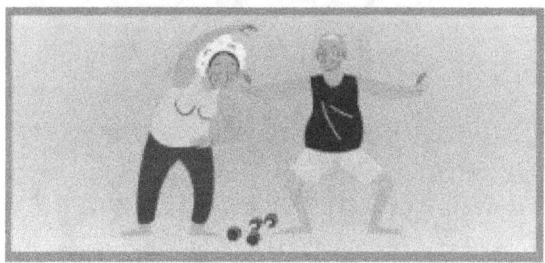

Your obsession weaves its tangled spell,

A charm both peculiar and unique,

Eyes upon me, they judge and compel,

Yet in their gaze, a love does peek.

This obsession's hold is fierce and
strong,

The eyes, they dance with mixed
emotion,

Displeasure lingers, a dissonant song,

But love persists, a powerful devotion.


Complaints rain down, like bitter
drops of rain,

Yet within them, a passion does reside,

The heart's desire, a flame that won't
wane,

Bound by this obsession, we cannot
hide.

Oh, how your obsession bewitches my
soul,

The eyes that pierce, both love and
resent,

In their gaze, mysteries begin to
unfold,

A paradoxical longing, heaven-sent.



We're caught in this web of desire,

Obsession's tendrils wrap tight around,

The eyes are our jury, set to inquire,

But love's flame burns, unyielding,
profound.

With every complaint, a touch of adoration,

The eyes reflect a love that won't subside,

This obsession's grip, a sweet temptation,

In its strange charm, we choose to confide.


Oh, how your obsession consumes my days,

The eyes both judge and cherish our plight,

In their gaze, a passionate haze,

A love entwined with shadows of night.

*So let the world question, let them inquire,*

*About this obsession we can't release,*

*For within its charm, our hearts conspire,*

*Bound by love's obsession, eternally at peace.*

**Chandan Malana**

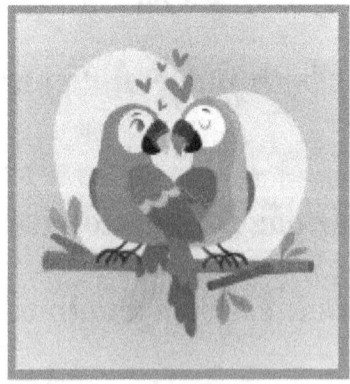

# Quote 33

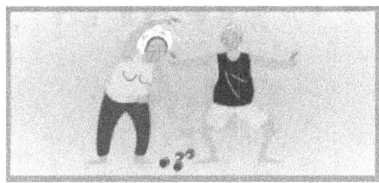

"My obsession for you, it never fades,
Like a flame that forever invades, Eyes
upon us, we remain unfazed, With
passion and love that never degrades."

Chandan Malana

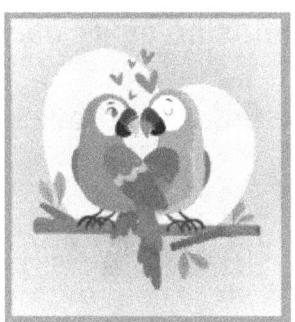

# Passion's Place: Where Hearts Take Flight

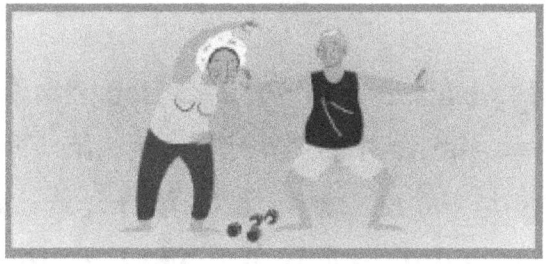

*Love doesn't judge by outer grace,*

*In hearts, its power finds its place,*

*Madness holds no sway over its game,*

*Appearance fades, but love remains the same.*

Obsession with looks can deceive the mind,

But true love's worth is hard to find,

It's not about faces, beauty or form,

But the depth of hearts, where love is born.


A pretty face may catch the eye,

But love's essence goes far and high,

It seeks the soul, the inner fire,

And ignites a love that will never tire.

In a world obsessed with the surface
shine,

Love sees beyond, a treasure to define,

It doesn't discriminate, it doesn't
judge,

Love embraces all, like a soothing
budge.



For love is not bound by physical grace,

It surpasses the limits of time and
space,

It's the connection of souls, the purest
of ties,

That brings two hearts together, under
love's skies.

Appearances may fade, wrinkles may form,

But love's flame burns bright, keeping hearts warm,

For it's not about looks, but the value within,

The love that's eternal, where true joy begins.


So, let go of the obsession with outer appeal,

Embrace the love that is real and surreal,

For love doesn't happen by looking at faces,

But by finding hearts where love embraces.

In the depths of hearts, love finds its true worth,

A love that transcends the boundaries of birth,

So let us cherish the beauty that's deep inside,

For that's where love resides, forever to abide.

Chandan Malana

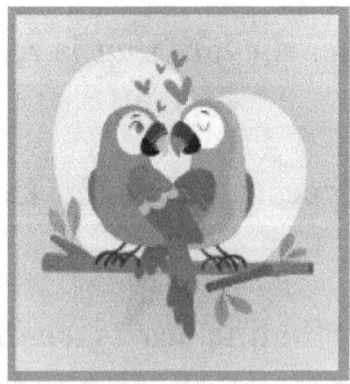

# Quote 34

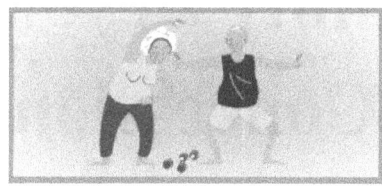

"Looks may charm, but can't sustain love's light, The madness of hearts is a celestial sight, Beyond mere appearances, it dwells out of sight, A place of passion, where hearts take flight."

*Chandan Malana*

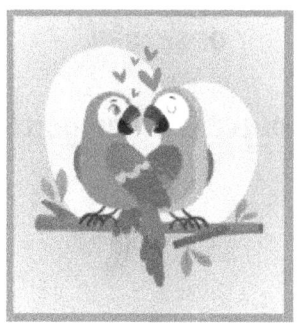

# Poetic Possession: Sanity Beyond Concession

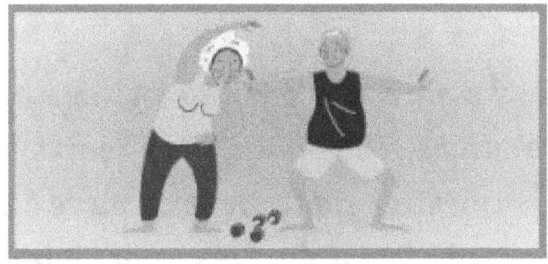

Life's troubles would be nothing more,

She declared with confidence galore,

"You're a poet, not insane, not obsessed,"

Words of solace, in her gentle address.

Amidst chaos, when turmoil grew,

She painted hope in colors anew,

Guiding me through the darkest nights,

Her belief in my words took flight.



In verses spun, my heart found peace,

Obsessions released, worries ceased,

For in the realm of poetic delight,

I found refuge, a respite from the fight.

In rhythm and rhyme, my soul's
release,

Each word a balm, granting me inner
peace,

The world's troubles faded, as poetry's
essence,

Brought solace, evoking profound
transcendence.


Through ink-stained pages, emotions
flowed,

Unburdened heart, a cathartic ode,

No longer confined by worries untold,

A poet's journey, no longer controlled.

With pen in hand, I embarked on a
quest,

To capture life's beauty, its every
bequest,

No longer plagued by obsessions of old,

I found freedom in verses, a story
untold.


Through metaphors and similes, I wove
my tale,

Escaping the confines of a troubled
trail,

She saw the poet in me, not a mind
deranged,

A healer of sorrows, my verses
exchanged.

So, I'll embrace this poetic reign,

For it grants solace in times of strain,

With confidence galore, I'll rise above,

Embracing my gift, fueled by her love.

**Chandan Malana**

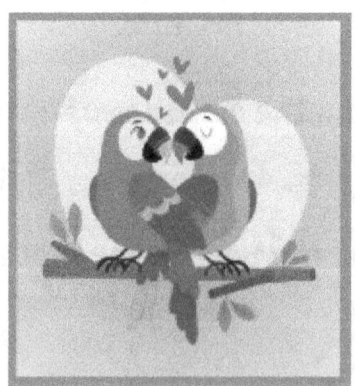

# Quote 35

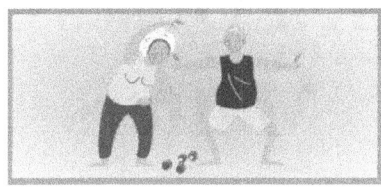

*"With confidence and poetic flair, She declared my sanity was beyond compare, For I was not insane nor was I obsessed, But simply a poet, and perhaps, just a little possessed."*

Chandan Malana

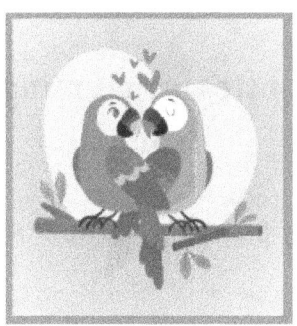

# Promises Scatter, When Obsession Matters

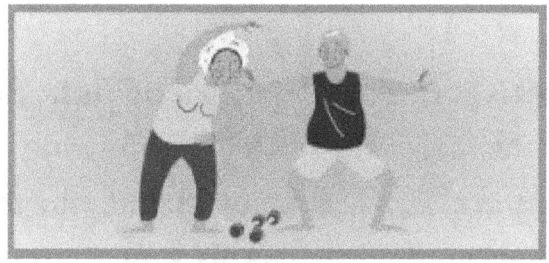

In the depths of fervent desire's
embrace,

Obsession blooms, with intensity and
grace.

Its flame ignites, consuming heart and
soul,

Unyielding passion, it seeks to control.

Obsession's gaze, unflinching, fixed
and sure,

Through veils of doubt, it dares to
endure.

Yet, in its wake, the promises do fade,

Empty oaths, like whispers, gently
degrade.

For obsession knows no bounds, nor
fear,

It feeds on dreams, each whispered
tear.

But false are the oaths, deceitful and
sly,

Their fragile facade, a clever disguise.

In its clutches, souls may find no rest,

Driven by hunger, an eternal quest.

Yet, in the shadows, truth does often
hide,

Deceptive promises, like shadows,
subside.



Obsession, a flame that burns within,

Kindling desires, both fervent and thin.

But the vows that bind, they often
deceive,

Leaving hearts shattered, unable to
believe.

So tread with caution, when obsession's near,

Its allure is enchanting, yet tinged with fear.

For false are the oaths, that may be spoken,

Obsession's truth, in secrets, stays unbroken.


Yet, through the haze, a lesson does emerge,

Obsession's grip, we must never splurge.

For in the end, it's the heart that must discern,

The falseness of promises, and passion's yearn.

Obsession may consume, with fiery desire,

But falsehoods, they kindle, then swiftly expire.

Look beyond the spell, with a discerning eye,

And let true love's light, your heart's path justify.

Chandan Malana

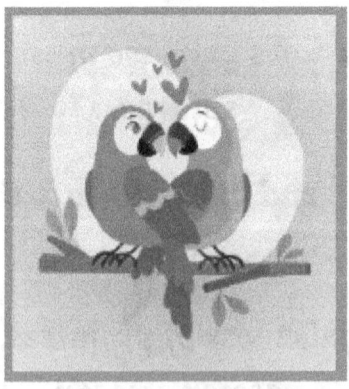

# Quote 36

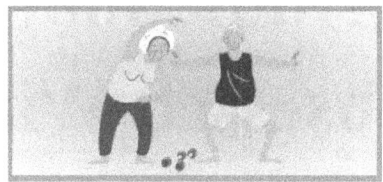

"A heart consumed by passion's flame,
Obsession's fire cannot be tamed, But
promises like ashes scatter, When false
oaths are all that matter."

*Chandan Malana*

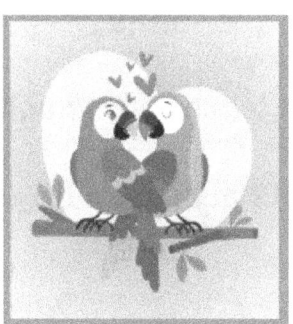

# Prose As Addiction, Obsessed With Your Fiction

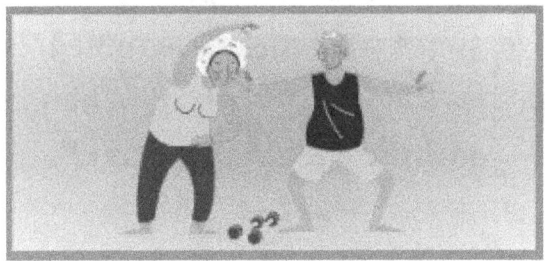

Write something that enchants the
mind,

A tale that leaves no thoughts behind.

Captivate my soul with words so
sweet,

A masterpiece that's hard to beat.

Craft a world of vivid dreams,

Where obsession flows in gentle streams.

Let passion ignite within my core,

With every line, I'll crave for more.


Whisper secrets in poetic verse,

Unleash desires, let them immerse.

Engage my senses, make me yearn,

For words that dance and freely churn.

Paint a picture with phrases rare,

An obsession I can't help but share.

Draw me in with your poetic art,

Leave an imprint on my longing heart.


Weave a tale of love's sweet embrace,

Fuel my obsession, let it race.

Through every stanza, make me sigh,

For words that make my spirit fly.

Sculpt emotions with each chosen word,

A symphony of feelings yet unheard.

Ignite the flames of longing deep,

In my obsession, let it seep.


Create a melody with lyrical grace,

A poem that time cannot erase.

Let me drown in its hypnotic trance,

With every verse, my obsession enhance.

Write something that makes me crave,

A poetic journey I can't escape.

Let me become lost within your rhyme,

Obsession ignited for all of time.

Chandan Malana

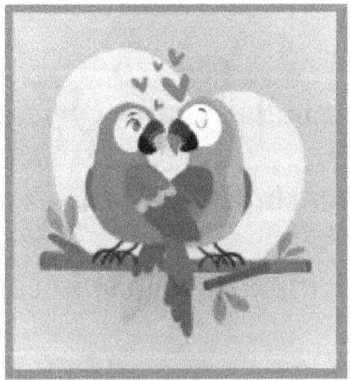

# Quote 37

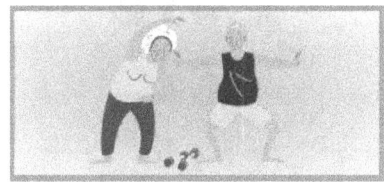

"Let my heart race with every word, As your prose becomes my world, Let your writing be my intoxication, A sweet obsession, my addiction."

Chandan Malana

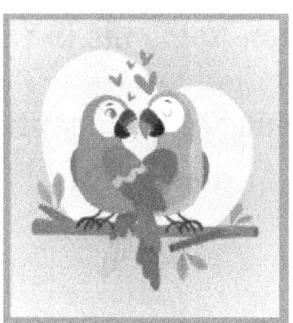

# Punishment Of Love

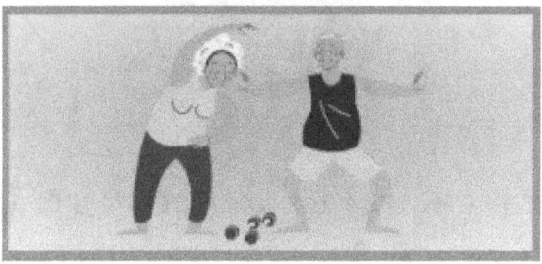

Since you made me crazy, lost in your gaze,

I'm a puppet, a prisoner, in this love-filled maze.

Every person holds me in their hands,

Bound by your spell, a captive of love's demands.

Even on his heart, intense love must
have passed,

For only such passion could make me
so steadfast.

The one who has imposed the
punishment of love,

I'm entangled, consumed, by emotions
above.

In every breath, your presence does
invade,

An obsession ignited, refusing to fade.

I long for your touch, your whispers in
my ear,

As I drown in desire, succumbing to
fear.

Your eyes, like magnets, pull me ever
near,

Entranced by their depth, overwhelmed
with sheer.

My thoughts are consumed by your
enchanting face,

Leaving no space for reason or escape.


I am but a vessel, filled with love's
obsession,

Lost in the waves of its relentless
aggression.

My heart beats wildly, a symphony of
desire,

Fueling this madness, this
unquenchable fire.

Every moment apart feels like eternity,

Yearning for the day when we're finally free.

But until then, I'll remain under your spell,

Caught in this whirlwind, where only you dwell.

You are the drug, the addiction I crave,

A love so intoxicating, it's impossible to save.

I surrender myself, willingly, to your power,

Bound to you, consumed, every waking hour.

Since you made me crazy, I've lost all control,

A slave to this passion, with nowhere to console.

But I'll cherish this madness, this love so profound,

For in its depths, a world of ecstasy is found.


Chandan Malana

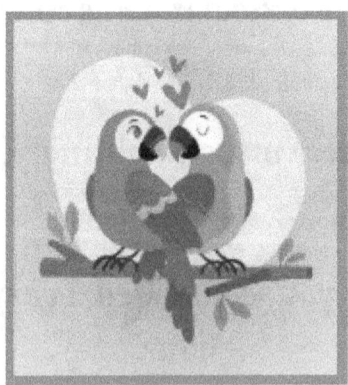

# Quote 38

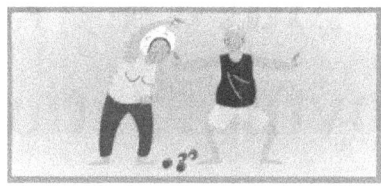

"Every soul I encounter holds me tight,
As if I'm some treasure, or lover's
delight. The one who made me crazy,
must have known, Of love's potency,
like a seed that was sown."

*Chandan Malana*

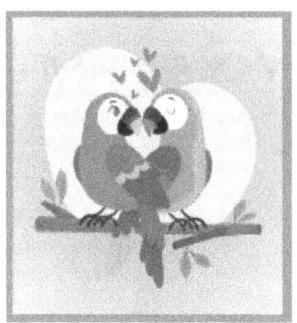

# Pure Adoration: In One-sided Love, A Joyful Elation

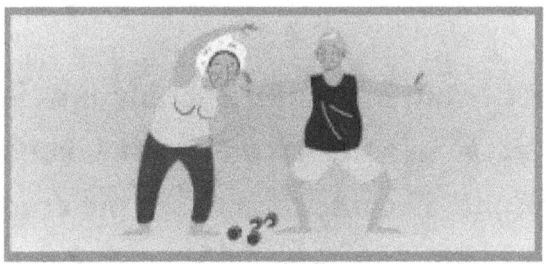

I'm delighted by this one-sided spell,

An obsession that no one can quell.

For though they may desire to sever,

This bond we share, it's mine forever.

A happiness deep within my soul,

This fixation, beyond their control.

No matter how hard they try and fight,

Our connection remains shining
bright.


Like a flame that dances with the
breeze,

This obsession brings me endless ease.

Their attempts to break us apart,

Are futile, for we're stitched heart to
heart.

In this one-sided love's embrace,

I find solace, a sacred space.

No matter what others may decree,

They cannot dissolve this bond with
me.




For in my heart, it firmly resides,

This obsession that I won't hide.

Its power and strength cannot be
undone,

As it glows brightly, like the rising sun.

Their skepticism cannot deter,

This one-sided love that I prefer.

It fuels my spirit, keeps me aflame,

In this bond, I find my rightful claim.


Through stormy skies or calmest seas,

This obsession remains my heart's
keys.

No matter what they may say or do,

I'm content with this love, tried and
true.

So let them question, let them doubt,

This one-sided obsession, devout.

For I know deep within my core,

This bond with myself, I'll forever
adore.

Chandan Malana

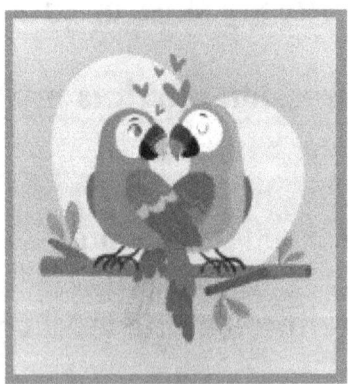

# Quote 39

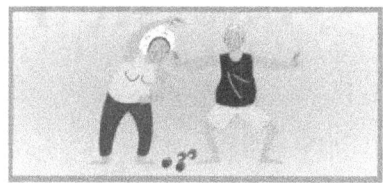

"*In my one-sided obsession, I find joy,
A love unrequited, yet not a ploy, For
even if they try, this bond won't sever,
My heart's devotion, a love that'll last
forever.*"

Chandan Malana

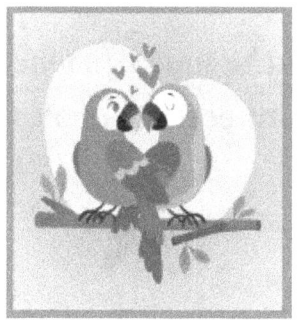

# Sacrifice Of Obsession

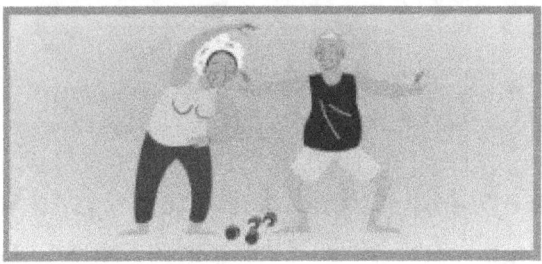

*In depths of longing, my heart was confined,*

*Obsession's chains, a prison of the mind.*

*But its demise, a sacrifice profound,*

*To breathe new life where true connections abound.*

With fervent ardor, I chased its elusive
grasp,

Blinded by desire, an all-consuming
gasp.

But now it lies, a memory so dear,

As I release its grip, love's essence
draws near.


From the ashes of my fixation's fall,

Sprout blossoms of devotion, strong
and tall.

No longer captive to a selfish plea,

I set my spirit free, love's harmony to
decree.

For in surrendering my obsession's
hold,

I find a sweeter melody, untold.

The sacrifices made were not in vain,

As new bonds flourish, like a summer
rain.


Once entangled in a web of desire,

Now liberated, my soul can aspire.

To nurture bonds with selfless care,

And mend the wounds that once
seemed unfair.

Obsession's suicide unveils the truth,

That love requires sacrifice, a precious
sleuth.

Its death has birthed a new beginning,

Where relationships bloom, a chance
for winning.




No longer shackled by a selfish plight,

I embrace the day, love's brilliant light.

For in letting go of what held me tight,

I discovered the power to make things
right.

*So let my obsession rest in peace,*

*Its sacrifice brings forth a love's increase.*

*And as I navigate life's winding road,*

*I'll cherish the connections that truly bestowed.*

Chandan Malana

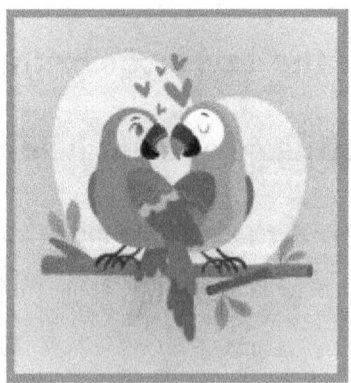

# Quote 40

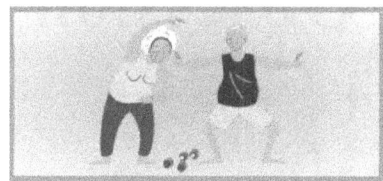

*"In the depths of my passion, I let go of my hold, For the sake of those connections, I relinquished control, And though it may seem like a tragic end, It became the starting point for new love to begin."*

Chandan Malana

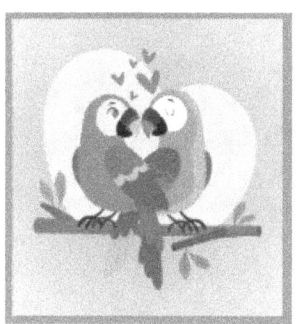

# Season Of Obsession

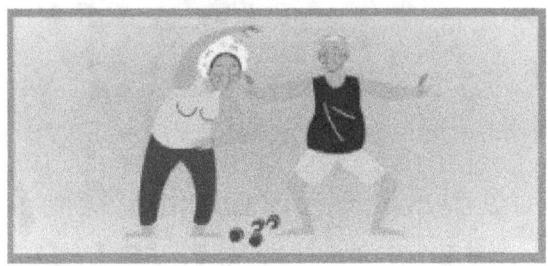

In shadows deep, the wounds do lie,

Scattered whispers of a love gone awry.

Their scent, a bittersweet perfume,

Drifting through the city, casting its gloom.

A broken heart's lament takes flight,

Obsession's tendrils, a haunting sight.

A season blooms with fervent desire,

Consuming souls with a relentless fire.


Within the streets, the wounds abide,

Their presence felt with every stride.

Aching echoes, like a mournful song,

The remnants of love that once
belonged.

Obsession's grasp, a tangled web,

Ensnaring hearts, leaving them
threadbare and dead.

Yet still, they yearn for love's embrace,

Lost in the depths of passion's chase.


The city pulses with a whispered plea,

As obsession spreads, like wildfire, free.

A dance of longing, a dangerous game,

Hearts entwined, forever marked by its
name.

Through shattered dreams and
shattered trust,

Obsession weaves its spell, turning love
to dust.

The wounds, they ache with a bitter
taste,

A testament to love's relentless haste.


But in the darkness, a flicker of light,

A chance for healing, to make things
right.

Though scars remain, their stories
told,

Hope whispers softly, in love's
stronghold.

So let the wounds, their fragrance bear,

For in their pain, new beginnings flare.

Obsession's season, both cruel and divine,

Teaches us to cherish love, one heartbeat at a time.

Chandan Malana

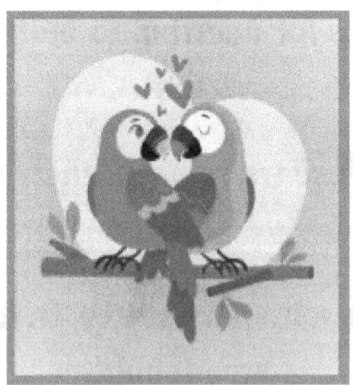

# Quote 41

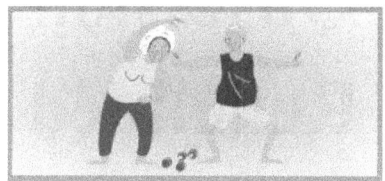

"The city's air is thick with a longing and pain, Like a symphony of heartbreak, it echoes in vain, The Obsession season is here, its scent in the breeze, A reminder that love's wounds never truly ease."

Chandan Malana

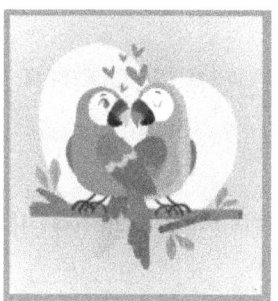

# Seasons Fled, Obsession Remained

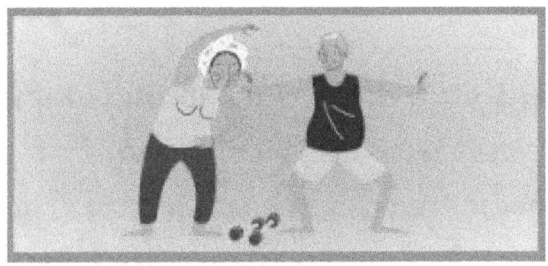

The seasons danced, their hues so
bright,

But tranquility waned, lost in the
night.

Obsession's grip tightened, hearts held
sway,

As life slipped away, fading day by day.

Gone are the days of peaceful embrace,

Now consumed by desires, a relentless chase.

Like a fire's blaze, devouring all in its wake,

What was lost, the ashes silently take.


Obsession's allure, a tempting mirage,

A haunting whisper, a siren's barrage.

What once was cherished now lost in its snare,

Leaving behind emptiness, a soul laid bare.

The blossoms withered, petals turned to dust,

As passion's flame consumed all in its thrust.

What was gained through obsession's blind spree?

A hollow victory, a mere phantom decree.


The seasons passed, their beauty fleeting,

Yet obsession lingered, its grip unrelenting.

Lost in the storm, the tranquil winds ceased,

Leaving behind a void, a heart in displease.

The sun's warm embrace now turned
bitter and cold,

As obsession's grasp tightened, a story
untold.

The joys of life faded, like colors in
decline,

Leaving behind regrets, etched in every
line.

In search of fulfillment, the soul
yearned,

But obsession's path only left it burned.

The seasons may change, but scars
remain,

A constant reminder of the relentless
pain.

So let us break free from obsession's chains,

Embrace the tranquility that still remains.

For life is a tapestry of moments, so vast,

Let us cherish each season, for they shall not last.

Chandan Malana

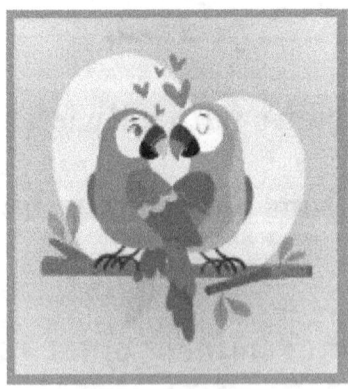

# Quote 42

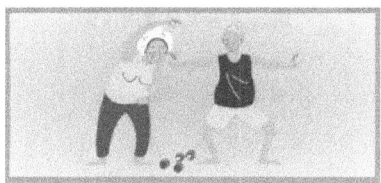

"Amidst the passing seasons and
fading tranquility, Lost in the sway of
an all-consuming Obsession's ability,
Life slips away like an ephemeral
dream, As Fire's blaze destroys all,
with an unstoppable gleam."

Chandan Malana

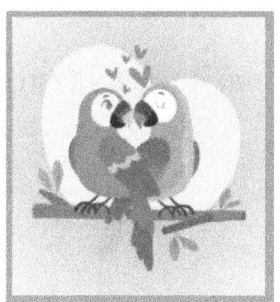

# Surpassing All Limits

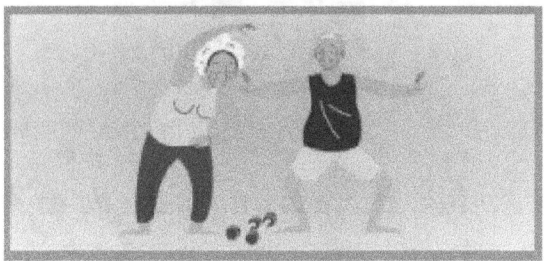

In obsession's grip, we'll take flight,

Bound by a love that burns so bright.

We'll transcend the realms of the ordinary,

And forge a path that's truly legendary.

With passion's flame, we'll set ablaze,

Our hearts entwined in an endless maze.

No boundaries or doubts shall ever sever,

For in our love, we'll endeavor.


I'll be the beat within your chest,

A rhythm that won't ever rest.

Together, we'll create a symphony,

A harmonious blend of you and me.

As breath, I'll gently touch your skin,

Whispering secrets, releasing within.

Our souls entangled, forever entwined,

In this obsession, our love defined.


In every moment, we'll strive for more,

Unleashing desires from our core.

No heights too high, no depths too
deep,

In this obsession, our souls will leap.

We'll dance on the edges of ecstasy,

Lost in a whirlwind of you and me.

No limits can bind us, we'll break free,

In this obsession, our love decree.



With every touch, a wildfire will ignite,

Burning fierce, shining so bright.

In this obsession, we'll rise above,

Discovering a love that's pure and true love.

*In the realm of obsession, we'll find our way,*

*Writing a tale no one else can portray.*

*Together, we'll create a love that's grand,*

*In this extraordinary bond, hand in hand.*

Chandan Malana

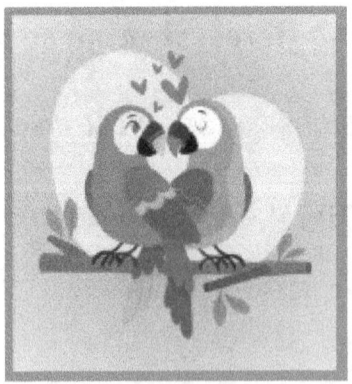

# Quote 43

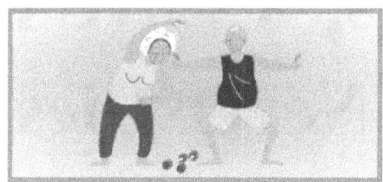

"In love's obsession, we shall soar,
Surpassing all limits like never before,
As your heart and beat, I shall become,
And as breath, I will come, our hearts
as one."

Chandan Malana

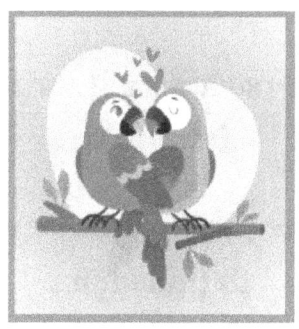

# The Fault Of Your Eyes, A Love That Never Dies

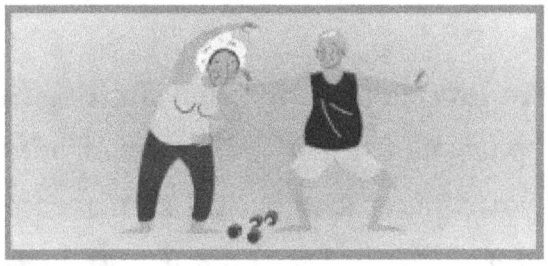

This is my Obsession, a fiery flame's reign,

An intoxication of love that consumes my brain,

If you don't recognize it, or fail to know its might,

Then it's the fault of your eyes, blinded to this sight.

A *passion so deep, it engulfs my very soul,*

*In its relentless grip, I am forever whole,*

No *escape from its grasp, no respite to find,*

*This obsession, this love, forever intertwined.*

*Like a siren's call, it beckons me near,*

*Drawing me closer, dispelling all fear,*

*In its enchanting embrace, I am lost and found,*

**Bound to this obsession, my heart knows no bounds.**

Every breath I take, every beat of my
heart,

Echoes the rhythm of this love, a
symphony's art,

It dances within me, a melody so sweet,

This intoxication of love, my soul's
eternal feat.

I'm consumed by desire, consumed by
its flame,

As this obsession engulfs me, I am not
the same,

It fuels my every thought, my every
dream,

This obsession, this love, an
unstoppable stream.

No boundaries can contain it, no walls
can confine,

This intoxication of love, an eternal
divine,

I surrender willingly, to its passionate
sway,

For in this obsession, I have found my
only way.


It's a whirlwind of emotions, a
tempest's roar,

Yet in its turbulence, I find solace and
more,

For this obsession, this love, has
become my guide,

Through the depths of my being,
forever it'll reside.

*So if you fail to understand, if you can't perceive,*

*The magnitude of this obsession, why I still believe,*

*Then know it's not my fault, nor yours to accuse,*

*For love's intoxication, only the heart can truly choose.*

Chandan Malana

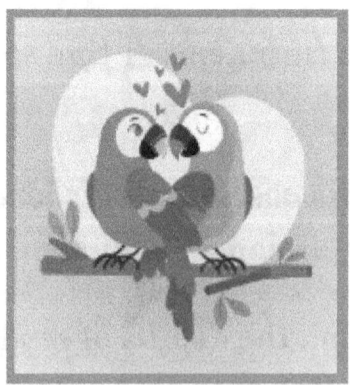

# Quote 44

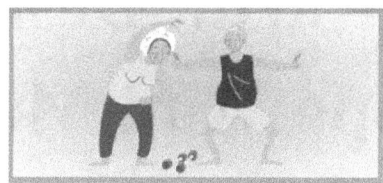

"My heart beats only for you, With an obsession that runs deep and true, If you fail to feel my love's sweet glow, Then it's your eyes that just don't know."

Chandan Malana

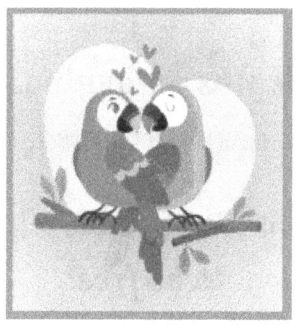

# Time's Due Reward: Desire, Hope, And More

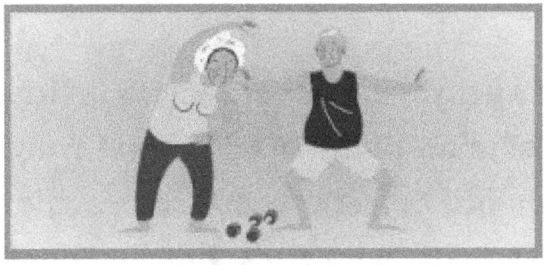

*Be it madness or intelligence, a mind's descent,*

*Obsession fuels the fire, with fervor so intense.*

*In the depths of longing, a soul's desperate plea,*

*To grasp what's beyond, what's meant to be free.*

With hope as our compass, we venture through the haze,

Seeking a path, through life's bewildering maze.

For in hope, we find solace, a beacon in the night,

Guiding us forward, towards a future bright.


Expectation dances, a restless, eager muse,

Whispering dreams, a symphony we can't refuse.

But patience we must learn, to let destiny unfold,

For time has its own rhythm, secrets yet untold.

Desire ignites, a flame within our
hearts,

Driving us onwards, tearing our
doubts apart.

With passion as our fuel, we reach for
the stars,

Embracing the chaos, and healing our
scars.


In madness, we find fragments of
truth,

Unveiling the depths of our
subconscious youth.

Through shattered illusions, we
glimpse the real,

Discovering hidden treasures, in
madness we reveal.

Intelligence guides, a sword to cut
through the noise,

Unraveling mysteries, with a mind
sharp and poised.

Knowledge is power, a key to unlock
the unknown,

Navigating the realms, where wisdom
is sown.


But only that which works out in due
time,

Becomes our own, in this grand
paradigm.

For the universe weaves its intricate
design,

Granting fruition, to the endeavors
divine.

So let us embrace the passions that drive,

Be it madness or intellect, let our spirits thrive.

With hope and expectation, let us dare to aspire,

For in the pursuit of dreams, we set our souls on fire.

Chandan Malana

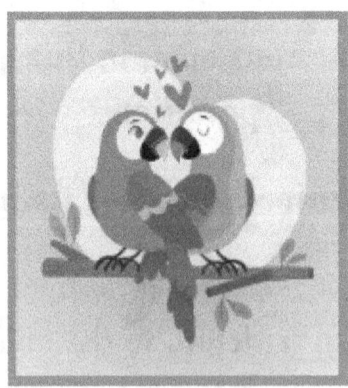

# Quote 45

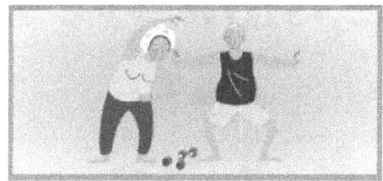

*"Madness, hope, intelligence, and more, All desires and expectations we explore. Yet only in time, can true ownership be gained, What's meant for us, will be ours, forever unchained."*

Chandan Malana

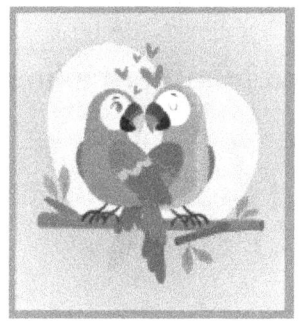

# Together In Obsession We Find

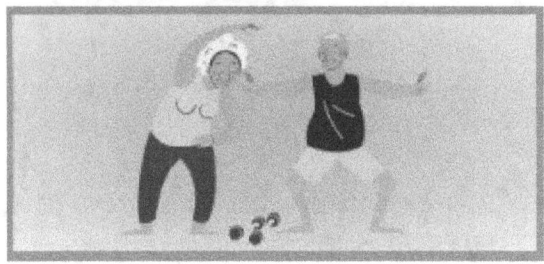

*There have come many to enlighten my mind,*

*To help me grasp what I once left behind.*

*Once alone in my obsession's domain,*

*Now joined by others who share this refrain.*

They speak of passions that burn deep within,

Of dreams and desires that never rescind.

Together we strive to uncover the truth,

In the depths of obsession, we find our youth.


Each one brings stories, their own tales to tell,

Of the times they've fallen under obsession's spell.

We gather as brethren, united by plight,

To chase our desires with all of our might.

Through words and through art, we
express our yearn,

A flame that within us will always
burn.

From painting to music, to writing
profound,

In our obsessions, creative treasures
are found.

We challenge each other to push the
bounds,

To dive into depths where obsession
resounds.

A collective force of minds intertwine,

To explore the mysteries of this
cherished shrine.

Though some may judge us, not fully aware,

Of the magic and wonder we ceaselessly share.

In our obsession, we find purpose and drive,

A passion that keeps our spirits alive.


We're not alone, as we once used to be,

A community formed, in obsession we see.

Supporting each other, we understand,

The power that comes from this fervent demand.

So let us embrace our obsessions, dear
friend,

For in them, a journey of self we
commend.

With others to guide us, together we
stand,

United, in this realm of the obsessed
man.

Chandan Malana

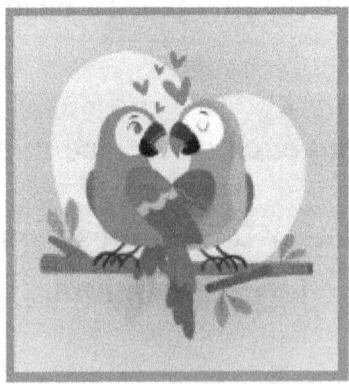

# Quote 46

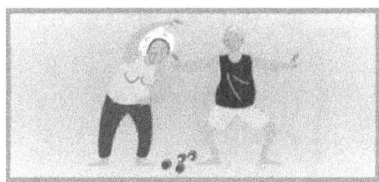

"My obsession was once a solitary flame burning bright, But as others saw its light, they too were drawn like moths in flight, Now we dance in its glow, a collective madness we call our own, And the fire of our passion burns brighter than ever known."

Chandan Malana

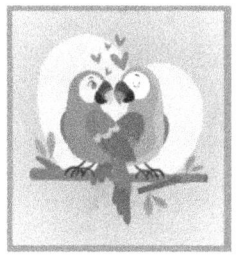

# Willing Surrender

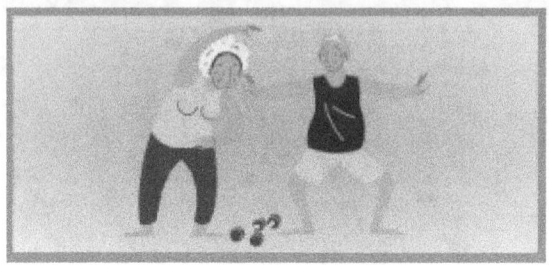

*In the depths of my soul, obsession resides,*

*A flame that burns, relentless and wide.*

*Though shattered and bruised, I'm still drawn to thee,*

*For in my brokenness, it's you I long to see.*

Like a moth to the flame, I'm helplessly
bound,

In your presence, solace and purpose
I've found.

Through trials and pain, my heart
remains true,

My obsession is unwavering, it's only
for you.


Whether fate allows our paths to
intertwine,

Or if we remain separated, worlds
apart, divine,

In my prayers, I beseech you, O
heavenly divine,

For your love, your guidance, eternally
I pine.

With each passing day, my longing grows,

A relentless yearning that only you know.

Obsessed, enchanted, consumed by your light,

In every breath I take, you're my sole delight.


Like a relentless seeker, I chase your grace,

Obsession's embrace, I cannot erase.

For in your presence, I find solace and peace,

In this world of chaos, my obsession won't cease.

*In dreams and fantasies, my heart is entwined,*

*With the image of you, my obsession defined.*

*No distance or time can erode this devotion,*

*It's you, only you, that stirs my soul's emotion.*


*From dawn till dusk, my thoughts revolve around you,*

*Obsession's tendrils, a love that's pure and true.*

*No matter the trials that life may bestow,*

*My obsession for you, forever it shall grow.*

So here I stand, a vessel of obsession,

Enraptured by your essence, lost in obsession.

In every breath I take, my heart beats for you,

Forever bound, my love, obsession's debut.

Chandan Malana

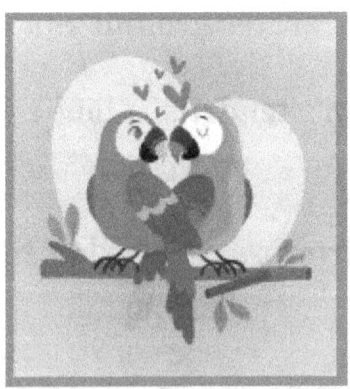

# Quote 47

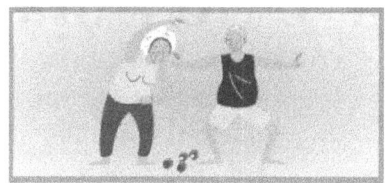

"My obsession runs deep, consumes my heart and soul, Even when shattered, my desire for you remains whole. In my heart, I yearn for your divine presence, In fervent prayer, I seek your loving essence."

Chandan Malana

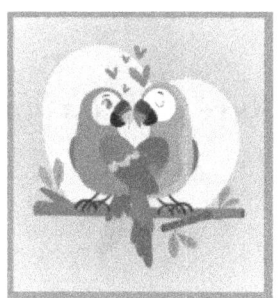

# Work Of Art, A Love So Smart

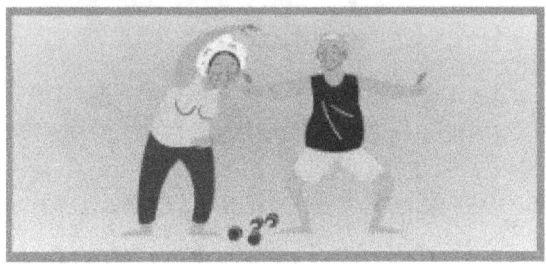

If love's your obsession, let it be
concealed,

A passion so potent, yet not easily
revealed,

Guard it within the chambers of your
soul,

For love's allure can consume and take
its toll.

As beasts are captivated by their
primal desires,

We, too, are drawn to love's burning
fires,

But restrain the yearning that lies
within,

Lest it consume you, and you cannot
begin.



For love's obsession can cloud the mind,

Blind us to reason, leaving us behind,

So keep it from the heart, hidden away,

Tread carefully, for obsession leads
astray.

Like a wild beast, love can mesmerize,

Intoxicating and enchanting, in
disguise,

But remember, dear heart, to stay in
control,

Lest you lose yourself in love's
relentless role.


Obsession breeds madness, a tempest
untamed,

A raging storm that leaves hearts
maimed,

So guard your love like a precious art,

And shield it carefully from the world's
depart.

Though passion may ignite and kindle the flame,

Beware the obsession that consumes in love's name,

For love should be gentle, a harmonious dance,

Not a destructive force, leaving little chance.


Let love bloom freely, but keep it in check,

Embrace its beauty, yet protect it from wreck,

For even the wildest of beasts can be tamed,

When love is cherished and not defamed.

So if you have a love for love, my dear friend,

Let it be a secret, until the time is right to send,

For love's obsession, though tempting and grand,

Must be handled with care, like a jewel in your hand.


Chandan Malana

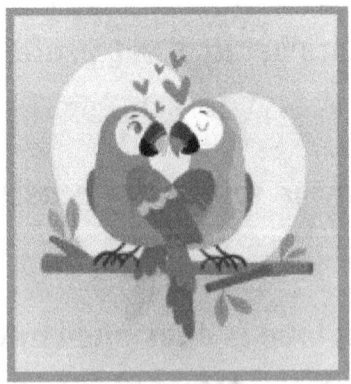

# Quote 48

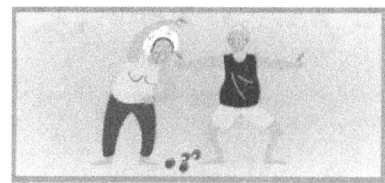

"Let love be more than just a feeling of
the heart, Let it be the light of your life,
a work of art, For when passion
consumes even the savage and wild, It's
not just a feeling, but a force that can
move and guide."

*Chandan Malana*

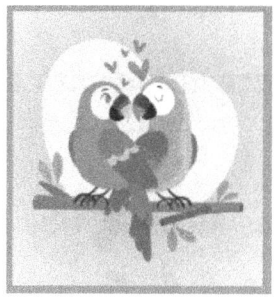

# Your Careless Love's Dagger

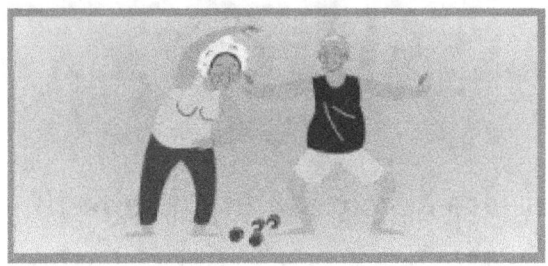

Making me crazy, you drift away,

Leaving me behind in disarray,

This feeling consumes my weary mind,

I've pleaded with you, but love, you're
blind.

Oh, don't gaze at me with that fervent
love,

For it drives me mad, like a wounded
dove.

Countless times I've voiced my desperate plea,

Begging you, darling, to set me free,

Yet you continue with your haunting stare,

A love so intense, it's too much to bear.

Oh, don't look at me with those adoring eyes,

For they ignite a fire I cannot disguise.

In this frenzy, my heart starts to ache,

An obsession born from love's cruel
stake,

You pull me closer, then push me away,

Leaving me longing, lost in dismay.

Oh, love of the world, I beg you, refrain,

From casting upon me this sweet
torment's chain.

Your affection traps me in a dizzy
haze,

Ensnared by emotions that never cease.

I've warned you, my dear, a hundred
times,

But still, you persist with your love's
chimes.

Oh, don't bestow upon me that
yearning gaze,

For it leaves me bewildered in a
haunting daze.

My sanity falters, my mind's in a spin,

This infatuation is the ultimate sin.

I yearn for solace, for a tranquil
reprieve,

But your love's grasp is too strong to
relieve.

Oh, love of mine, please heed my plea,

Release me from this captivating
decree.

The world spins around, as I'm left behind,

By your love's madness, I'm confined.

I've pleaded with you, oh, countless times,

To spare me the torment, the delirious rhymes.

Oh, don't ensnare me with your amorous charms,

For they fuel the fire, igniting my alarms.

In this labyrinth of desire, I'm lost,

Tangled in emotions, the ultimate cost.

I've warned you, my love, a hundred
times,

Yet you persist with these affectionate
crimes.

Oh, turn away from me, with love
untold,

Let this madness cease, release its
stronghold.

I've reached the brink, I can take no more,

This obsession has left my heart sore.

Don't gaze at me with love's bewitching spell,

For it pushes me deeper into this hell.

Oh, love of mine, please set me free,

Break these chains and let my spirit flee.

Chandan Malana

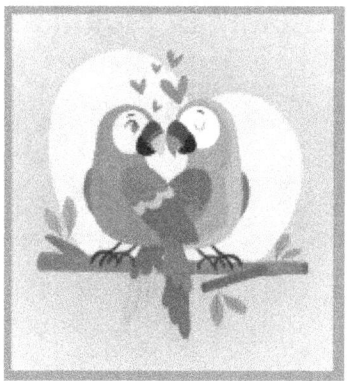

# Quote 49

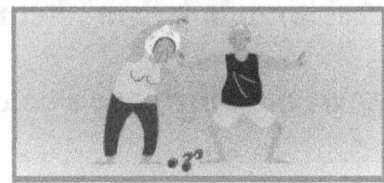

*"The pain of heartbreak, a constant refrain, Echoing through my mind again and again, Your careless love, like a dagger in my chest, A reminder that true affection is just a quest."*

Chandan Malana

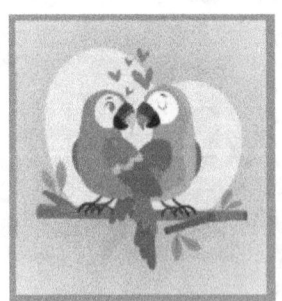

# You're The Sun In My Sky

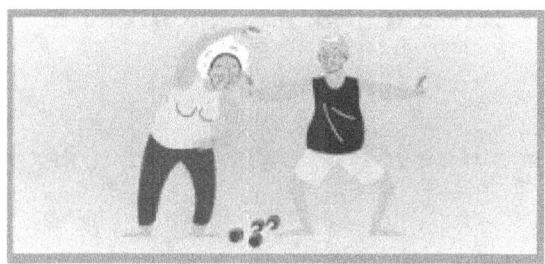

You are my life's companion, dear and true,

In this journey, my love, it's only me and you.

Your presence fills my heart with delight,

A bond so strong, it feels just right.

Your fragrance lingers in my every
breath,

A sweet aroma, defying life and death.

Like sandalwood, you grace my
dreams,

A scent that lingers, forever it seems.


Even now, your beauty leaves me in
awe,

Each glance, each smile, an enchanting
draw.

Your eyes sparkle like stars in the
night,

Guiding my path with their radiant
light.

Your charm, my love, drives me to the edge,

An obsession that has me firmly pledged.

Your laughter echoes in my every thought,

A melody that cannot be unfraught.


In your embrace, I find solace and peace,

A sanctuary where all worries cease.

Your touch ignites flames within my soul,

A burning desire I cannot control.

Every moment spent with you is a
treasure,

A bond so strong, it knows no measure.

You are the rhythm that beats in my
heart,

An eternal love, never to depart.

In your presence, my beloved, I find
bliss,

A love that's pure, a never-ending kiss.

Together, we dance to love's sweet
symphony,

Bound by a love that defies all
scrutiny.

You are my life's companion,
forevermore,

In your arms, I've found what I've been
searching for.

With you, my love, I'll always be,

For you are my life's greatest ecstasy.

**Chandan Malana**

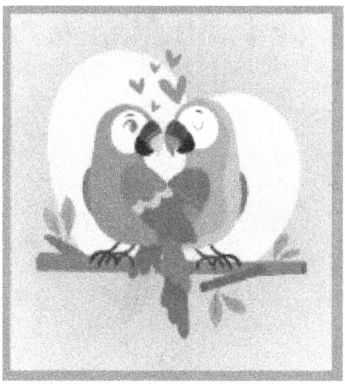

# Quote 50

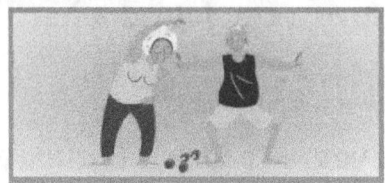

"You're the sun in my sky, the stars in
my night, With you, my beloved,
everything feels so right. Your presence
in my life is like a beautiful dream,
With you by my side, everything
glimmers, and nothing is as it seems."

**Chandan Malana**

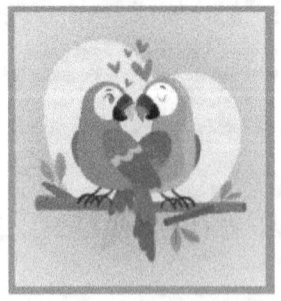

# Buy Me A Cup Of Coffee

**Dear readers,**

Thank you so much for taking the time to read my words. If I have in some way managed to touch your life, then I am truly honoured.

I hope that my poetry and words have been able to time travel you back to any emotion and in some way, some where, somehow, in some place, in some moment touched your life then my life has become purposeful for others.

If you have enjoyed my work and would like to show your appreciation, I would be delighted if you could buy me a cup of coffee. Your support would mean the world to me. Every bit helps and I am truly grateful for your generosity. Thank you once again,


Your faithful writer


**Chandan Malana**

# Paytm, Google pay, Phonepe, UPI

## chandan.malana@paytm

\*\*\*\*\*\*

## paypal.me/ChandanMalana

\*\*\*\*\*\*

chandanmalana@gmail.com

\*\*\*\*\*\*

instagram.com/chandan_malana

\*\*\*\*\*\*

# EUR account details

Account holder: Chandan Malana
SWIFT/BIC: TRWIBEB1XXX
IBAN: BE75 9674 9601 8051
Wise's address:
Avenue Louise 54, Room S52
Brussels
1050
Belgium

******

# GBP account details

## GBP Outside the UK

**Account holder: Chandan Malana**
**SWIFT/BIC: TRWIGB2L**
**IBAN: GB71 TRWI 2314 7012 4893 22**
**Wise's address:**
**56 Shoreditch High Street**
**London**
**E1 6JJ**
**United Kingdom**

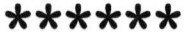

# GBP Inside the UK

Account holder: Chandan Malana
Sort code: 23-14-70
Account number: 12489322
IBAN: GB71 TRWI 2314 7012 4893
22
Wise's address:
56 Shoreditch High Street
London
E1 6JJ
United Kingdom

******

# USD account details

Account holder: Chandan Malana
ACH and Wire routing number:
084009519
Account number:
9600010468802671
Account type: Checking
Wise's address:
30 W. 26th Street, Sixth Floor
New York NY 10010
United States

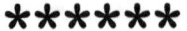

# BSC
# BNB Smart Chain
# [BEP20]

**0x652347bc8ccbe876a1cd93534a1
8c6d4b7bd4d8f**

# Books By This Author

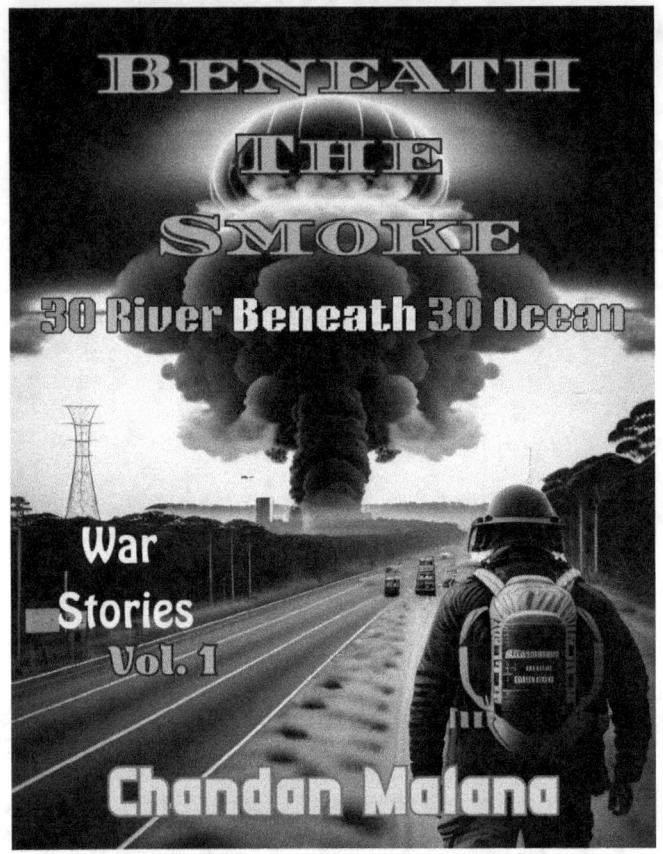

## Beneath The Smoke

### 30 River Beneath 30 Ocean

### War Stories

### Vol. 1